Light from the Mountain

Norlan Scrudder

Parson's Porch & Company

Parson's Porch Books

Light from the Mountain

ISBN: Softcover 978-1-949888-60-7

Copyright © 2014 by Norlan Scudder

All rights reserved. No part of this book may be reproduced or transmitted in any form or by any means, electronic or mechanical, including photocopying, recording, or by any information storage and retrieval system, without permission in writing from the publisher.

To order additional copies of this book, contact:

Parson's Porch Books

1-423-475-7308

www.parsonsporch.com

Parson's Porch Books is an imprint of Parson's Porch & Company (PP&C) in Cleveland, Tennessee. PP&C is an innovative non-profit organization which raises money by publishing books of noted authors, representing all genres. All donations from contributors and profits from publishing are shared with the poor.

Table of Contents

Searching for God   5
    Jeremiah 29:10-14

Hope after Devastation   12
    I Kings 19

Go! Sow Seeds   22
    Matthew 13:1-9

Led by the Spirit   30
    Acts 2:14-21

Our Friend, the Church   40
    Acts 11:19-26

Ashes, the Sign of the Cross   46
    Matthew 26:36-41

What Happens Next?   52
    Luke 8; Matthew 13

Courage to Live by Faith   59
    1 Corinthians 13 (NIV)

Light from the Mountain   68
    Luke 9: 28-42

Standing on the Promises   74
    Nehemiah 8:1-4 (RSV)

Blessed are Those Who Believe…   80
    John 12:1-8

God Leads Us Along   87
    Mark 4:35-41

The Church…At the Gates of Hell   93
    Matthew 16:13-20

Jesus, the Shepherd King　　　　　　　　　　　　　　　100
　　　Matthew 25:31-46

Take Care of What God Gives You　　　　　　　　　105
　　　Joshua 24:13-17 (NIV)

Behold the Lamb of God　　　　　　　　　　　　　111
　　　Revelation 1:4-8

Searching for God
Jeremiah 29:10-14

10. For thus says the Lord: After seventy years are completed at Babylon, I will visit you and perform my good word toward you, and cause you to return to this place.
11. For I know the thoughts that I think toward you, says the Lord, thoughts of peace and not of evil, to give you a future and a hope.
12. Then you will call upon me and go and pray to me, and I will listen to you.
13. And you will seek me and find me, when you search for me with all your heart.
14. I will be found by you, says the Lord, and I will bring you back from your captivity; I will gather you from all the nations and from all the places where I have driven you, says the Lord, and I will bring you to the place from which I cause you to be carried away captive.

People everywhere…..
    Whether or not they know it…. Are searching
    Searching…searching for something that satisfies
    Their need for:
        Knowledge
            Direction
        Answers to the age old questions
        Happiness and Satisfaction………..

This age has more….
    Appreciates it less
        And is more restless than any age before us.

Appetites are never satisfied
    Questions are never answered
        Lives are in shambles….
            Family Relationships are broken
And ………….
    I believe there are more abused children…
        More gang related deaths…
            Than ever before

SO…. WHAT IN THE WORLD IS WRONG????

Scriptural Background

The Children of Israel has sinned against God so grievously that God had allowed their old enemy to capture them and drag them off into Babylon (BAGDAD, IRAQ)….

God sent a messenger to them to explain what would take place as they were hauled off in chains…
The letter was delivered to the people by God's servant EL-A-SAH… (We say, Elisha).

God tells them that He was the one who sent them into captivity and that they would be there until they had a change of mind, heart and soul…

God also tells them not to listen to the false prophets… the soothsayers….

Today's Reading

You're going to be there for 70 years… a long time but time for the old sinners who got you into this mess to die out…

THEN……. After 70 years I will visit you and instill my words into your hearts again …

BUT THERE WILL BE A REQUIREMENT….

THEN… You will call upon me and pray to me and I will listen……

You shall seek me and find me when you search for me with your whole heart…

Think about it!

So what does all of this have to do with us here today?

Every Age has asked:
    Where is God?
    Is there a God?

If there is a God…. Why does He allow all this bad
            stuff to happen?
AND……….. Why doesn't He just come back and Put
            things right?

***

STORY………. ABOUT New York City

 (Has nothing to do with picante sauce)….

A Lady died and left a strange will…. All her wealth, she left to God…

Attorneys actually tried to comply…
        Would they give it to a church?
                A Charitable Organization…
 But… they couldn't come to an agreement.

SO…….. A JUDGE INSTRUCTED THEM TO GO THROUGH THE LEGAL REQUIRED "SEARCH FOR GOD".

        God was named as Party of the first part…
        God was summonsed to appear and claim the
            inheritance.
        Newspaper ads were published….
            30 days' notice was given for God to show up.

BUT WHEN GOD DID NOT SHOW UP… THAT JUDGE DECLARED THAT GOD COULD NOT BE FOUND IN NEW YORK CITY ……..
            AND SO THE CITY GOT ALL OF THE
        MONEY AND PROPERTY…

(That was before 9-11)

AFTER THAT TERRIBLE DAY…
    MANY PEOPLE FOUND GOD WALKING WITH
    THEM IN THE STREETS OF NY CITY…

Just as people did after the bombing of the Murray building in OKC

***

NOW REMEMBER OUR SCRIPTURE?
(I like the KJV)
Jeremiah 29:13

"Ye shall seek me and find me, when...
.... YOU SHALL SEARCH FOR ME
...WITH ALL YOUR HEART"

Jeremiah is a message of HOPE!

When Israel has sinned so grievously that there was no salvation for them, God allowed their sinful neighbor Babylon to conquer them and take them off into 70 years of slavery...

But God Promised that God still loved them and would again offer them a chance for Salvation... but it all depended on them...
"IF YOU WILL SEARCH FOR ME
WITH ALL YOUR HEARTS...
I'LL BE THERE".

***

PLEASE REMEMBER
THE MESSAGE IS EVERYWHERE
Even in their Babylonian captivity God was there.
(Babylon...is really BAGDAD).

To those of us who believe in God,
God is everywhere and can be seen in everything and everyone around us.
God is revealed in:
Nature.... Sunset, fruit, birds, even wild animals
People... (Sometimes you have to look pretty hard to

see god in people these days… but God is there.

GOD IS AS NEAR AS THE NEXT BREATH YOU TAKE…

***

STORY…

Years ago I was pastor of a large old downtown church in Evansville, Indiana. The church community had deteriorated greatly and those large old three story homes had been filled up with hippies and druggies of the 70's…

The Church…
Had made a commitment to stay, even though we were building a New Church (a satellite church) in the suburbs, many would stay until the doors closed or they were able to reach that community.

Have you ever gone to a funeral for a Church?
We went back 2006…

> In the early 70's that church had 500 regular, dedicated members but in 2006 they closed their doors…No longer able to keep ministry going
> No longer able to keep up that gorgeous Old building…

***

I knew they had tried desperately to keep up their commitment to bring in that neighborhood but everything they tried and prayed for seemed to be a failure. **It Wasn't!**

I REMEMBER TWO PEOPLE who showed all the rest of us
What it meant to let others see Jesus in you… and in that church community that had turned into a "hippy community".

Merium: taught a woman's bible study group and had gathered about 20 of those hippie type women, living in those dingy apartments, some on drugs, others had just decided to drop out...

But not everyone in the community liked Merium teaching the Bible to those young women...

Some of their husbands or live-in boyfriends resented their Ladies "getting religion"... and lives were changed.

So... they threatened Merium... but she kept on
They beat her up and took her money... but she kept on.
They broke her arm and put her in the hospital... but she didn't quit.
(She kept that Bible class going until the very end).

I remember TOM...
He was (or looked like) the hippiest of hippies...
Tom was a devout Christian. He wouldn't tell you much about himself... <u>Only that Jesus had saved him</u>.

When he would come to my office we would talk about how to reach those drop-out kids... but he had the only answer to that.. BE ONE OF THEM.... AND HE WAS.

THE ONLY THING TOM WANTED WAS FOR US TO FURNISH HIM COPIES OF THE SCRIPTURES IN MODERN LANGUAGE... WE DID!

He would <u>not</u> take money... not even a meal, but he would use our Gym to play with some basketball with some of the kids, take a shower and go back to living on the streets.

When the Church gets serious about letting others see Jesus in us... we will not have empty halls and empty buildings.... And... we have to be willing to get our beautiful buildings considerably messed up.

How, then, do WE find God?

JUST LOOK AT WHERE PEOPLE FOUND JESUS…

    Sometimes arguing with the Pharisees, but sometimes sitting down at their table…

    Touching the dirty lepers…
        Lifting a prostitute from the dust and telling her to Go and sin no more…

    In inviting himself to the house of Zacchaeus the hated tax collector (IRS agent).

    In a boat… threatened by a storm

    In the Desert of Temptation
        Or…. Feeding thousands with five loaves and two fish……….

    In the streets of the hated Samarians
        (And with the woman at the well)

    They found him at a wedding banquet… He was not a prude.

HOW DOES OUR GENERATION OF SCATTERED PEOPLE FIND GOD?

PERHAPS IT IS WHEN THEY SEE THE CHURCH BEING THE HANDS AND FEET OF JESUS OR EVEN…..

…..When they see Jesus in you………

AND……When they shall search for Him with all their hearts…

Now let me speak plainly to Duncan CP Church…

    You can't put ministry…

Outreach to new people
Or church growth on hold…

UNTIL YOU CAN RELOCATE
OR GET A NEW BUILDING….

Never give up… never quit… keep reaching out to new people who are in need of searching for God…AND….

Let us renew our search. AMEN!

Hope after Devastation
Elijah and Elisha
I Kings 19

2. Then Jezebel sent a messenger unto Elijah, saying, so let the gods do to me, and more also, if I make not thy life as the life of one of them by tomorrow about this time.

3. And when he saw that, he arose, and went for his life, and came to Beersheba, which belongs to Judah, and left his servant there.

4. But Elijah went a day's journey into the wilderness, and came and sat down under a juniper tree: and he requested for himself that he might die; and said, it is enough; now, O Lord, take away my life; for I am not better than my fathers.

9. ... Elijah came to a cave, and lodged there; and behold, the word of the Lord came to him, and he said to him, "What are you doing here, Elijah?"

10. He said, "I have been very <u>zealous</u> for the Lord, the God of hosts; for the people of Israel have forsaken thy covenant, thrown down thy altars, and slain thy prophets with the sword; and I, even I only, am left; and they seek my life, to take it away."

11. And God said, "Go forth, and stand upon the mount before the Lord." And behold, the Lord passed by, and a great and strong wind rent the mountains, and broke in pieces the rocks before the Lord, but the Lord was not in the wind; and after the wind an earthquake, but the Lord was not in the earthquake;

12. And after the earthquake a fire, but the Lord was not in the fire; and after the fire a still small voice.

13. And when Elijah heard it, he wrapped his face in his mantle and went out and stood at the entrance of the cave. And behold, there came a voice to him, and said, "What are you doing here, Elijah?"

18. Yet I will leave seven thousand in Israel, all the knees that have not bowed to Baal, and every mouth that has not kissed him."

19. So he departed from there, and found Elisha the son of Shaphat, who was plowing, with twelve yoke of oxen before him, and he was with the twelfth. Elijah passed by him and cast his mantle upon him.

20. And he left the oxen, and ran after Elijah, and said, "Let me kiss my father and my mother, and then I will follow you." And he said to him, "Go back again; for what have I done to you?"

21. And he returned from following him, and took the yoke of oxen, and slew them, and boiled their flesh with the yokes of the oxen, and gave it to the people, and they ate. Then he arose and went after Elijah, and ministered to him.

Let me speak a Prophetic word from the pages of the Old Testament that resound with powerful truths for today.

Our world is filled with devastation. The news keeps us on our spiritual toes wondering where and what the next disaster will be, but in the midst of all this is the Church of Jesus Christ, our Lord.

Our first calling is to place the mantle of the priesthood, and the calling of disciples, upon the shoulders of the next generation of servants.

Tornadoes, Fires, Earthquakes and Wars engulf us and we try, ever so much to minister to these hurts, but a quick look into church history reveals that there are many peaks and valleys for the ministries and witness of the church.

Good times and bad times

    Times of great success

        And times of great loss and failure.

Elijah…was the same… He had great success against the enemy of Almighty God… then he was driven to despair when his life was threatened.

Since the time of Jesus….

    The church has been victorious…

    Then encountered the worst times of failure...

Surely… We understand that we are going through just a time for all of Christianity today…

    We experienced a time of growth after WW-II

    Only to "Sin Away Our Day of Grace"….

***

Dr Virgil Todd, (Professor of OT at Memphis Theological Seminary, and also Cumberland Presbyterian Theological Seminary when it was on campus of Bethel College in Mc- Kenzie TN), Warned all of his students that there was a great cycle

Found in the Old Testament that we seem doomed to repeat….

He called it the FORD theory.

    F - When Israel had been given everything they
        Soon **FORGOT** God and worshiped Idols of   BAAL.
    O - **OPPRESSION** God allowed evil neighbors to
Conquer them and take them away into slavery.
    R - Out of desperation they would return to God in
    REPENTENCE, and God would save them
From their enemies...
    D - **DELIVERENCE** came only when they returned to
        God and they would once again be returned to their
        homes to worship the living God, not idols.

It would be interesting to know just where we think we are in the church of today…. In that repetitive cycle….

    Take a Look at:

        Our Church

        Our Nation

        World-Wide Christianity

It seems to me that the cycle is playing out in every Church,

    Every Denomination

        And… Every Nation in the world…

***

The Story of Elijah the Tishbite

Elijah was a prophet in a time when all of Israel had forsaken God and they were again worshiping BAAL…

    King Ahab and Queen Jezebel had led the people to do just

        That…. And they hated TRUTH…

Elijah …. Brought the unfaithful people of Israel to Mount Carmel and challenged 450 evil prophets of BAAL

    To a contest...

<u>Verse 23</u>. Let them therefore give us two bulls; and let them choose one bull for themselves, and cut it in pieces, and lay it on wood, and put no fire under: and I will dress the other bullock, and lay it on wood, and put no fire under:

24. And call you on the name of your gods, and I will call on the name of the Lord: and the God that answers by fire, let him be God. And all the people answered and said, it is well spoken.

The FOLLOWERS OF BAAL PRAYED all morning for their false gods to send down fire to consume their calf...

    They danced,

        Cried... cut themselves,

            Until they fell into exhaustion...

<u>NOTHING HAPPENED</u>

    All THE WHILE Elijah made fun of them...

        All day... where is your god...

           Sleeping... on a journey... talking?

***

<u>ELIJAH</u> had the Israelites to Rebuild the Altar of the Lord

    He placed a sacrifice to be burned on the Altar

THEN at evening...ELIJAH PRAYED.... (Chapter 18:37-38)

        Remember they had laid 12 stones

        Put on wood and barrels of water

        Seemingly to make it impossible to burn

Elijah's Prayer

Hear me, O Lord, hear me, that this people may know that YOU are the Lord God, and that YOU have turned their heart back again.

Then the fire of the Lord fell, and consumed the burnt sacrifice, and the wood, and the stones, and the dust, and licked up the water that was in the trench.

The Prophets of BAAL fled but all 450 of them were killed...

And the People turned away from the false gods.

The draught of several years was broken and Rain fell and their land was refreshed and God blessed the people who returned to Him.

TROUBLE

KING AHAB... had witnessed it all and instead of believing and acting himself he goes directly to **JEZABEL...**

WHO IMMEDIATELY THREATENS THE LIFE OF ELIJAH.

Elijah who had been so victorious at Mt. Carmel now became the coward.

He fled into the desert and sleeps under a Juniper three and asks God to take his life....

> God scolds him and sends him 40 days journey
>
> Where He takes refuge in a cave...

God Called to Elijah...from the cave....

ELIJAH answered God with these words:

> **"I, even I only, am left; and they seek my life, to take it away."**

11. And God said, "Go forth, and stand upon the mount before the Lord." And behold, the Lord passed by, and a great and strong wind rent the mountains, and broke in pieces the rocks before the Lord,

but the Lord was not in the wind; and after the wind an earthquake, but the Lord was not in the earthquake;

12. And after the earthquake a fire; but the Lord was not in the fire: and after the fire a still small voice.

NOTE: How about that still small voice... can you find a place of?

      Silence to listen to that small voice today? Are you listening?

13. And it was so, when Elijah heard it, that he wrapped his face in his mantle, and went out, and stood in the entering in of the cave. And, behold, there came a voice unto him, and said,

What doest thou here, Elijah? GO TO WORK

   GET OUT OF HERE...

SO ELIJAH GOES AND FINDS THE NEXT GENERATION TO FOLLOW IN HIS FOOTSTEPS...

    ELISHA... PLOWING IN A FIELD

Note: This young man is plowing in a field following several teams of oxen and Elijah slips the Priestly Mantle on him, and his life changed forever.

MESSAGES FOR TODAY...

So how does all of this story translate into a meaningful lesson for the church of the 21st century?

Where are we in the cycle of things..........?

    Are we falling Away from God?

    Are we starting our time of punishment?

    Are Repentant ....?

We have fled into our Caves

It seems to me that the Church of today is:

    Licking our wounds from losses

        Crawling into our caves and

            We are afraid to speak out …….

Can't even display the Ten Commandments,

    Or Say a Prayer at a football game

While recently, A SCHOOL HAD A SPECIAL ASSEMBLY TO ALLOW MUSLUMS TO EXPLAIN WHY EVERYONE SHOULD BE A MUSLUM

    And the Assembly was Compulsory……..

                ***

        So……..Where is the Hope?

God Calls Us OUT OF OUR CAVES TO SEE WHAT IS HAPPENING

<u>GOD SAYS AGAIN:</u> Yet I have left me seven thousand in Israel, all ON their knees which have not bowed unto Baal,

The main-line traditional Church is shrinking in the US Today…

    We fight among ourselves over nothing…

(Perhaps because someone moved the piano from where it had been for fifty years without asking the session)

Now people are leaving the church to gravitate to larger more affluent churches that have programs and events for every kind of ministry.

TODAY………

One Church I know well, will decide today whether to keep paying pastor's salary….Or make building payments instead. It would be easy for us to THROW IN THE TOWEL…BUT Wait….

We have Missionary work in: (Sent from our Board of Missions…)

Humanitarian work in

    Kyrgyzstan, Japan, China, Nepal, South Korea, Colombia, Mongolia, Cambodia, Brazil, Myanmar, Guatemala, Mexico, Zambia, and Uganda.

Established Churches in Japan, China, South Korea, Laos, the Philippines, Colombia, and Brazil.

GOD SENDS US OUT TO PLACE THE MANTLE UPON

    THE NEXT GENERATION OF BELIEVERS

***

Today is World-Wide Communion Sunday

As we gather about this table let us know that we join with our Brothers and Sisters all around the world…

More than that Holy Communion is CELEBRATED

    IN HUNDREDS OF DENOMINATIONS

        HERE IN THE USA

            AND AROUND THE WORLD

Elijah thought he was the only one in the world who still loved and served God… but he was wrong.

> **There were 7,000 in Israel who had not bowed to Baal.**

When we look at World-Wide Christianity…

    When we see the Global growth of Christianity

WE KNOW WE **ARE PASSING THE MANTLE…**

NOW…. It is time for us to bring others into the worship and service of Jesus Christ, our Lord, here and around the world.

    AMEN!

Go! Sow Seeds
Matthew 13:1-9

On the same day Jesus went out of the house and sat by the sea. And great multitudes were gathered together to Him, so that He got into a boat and sat; and the whole multitude stood on the shore.

3. Then He spoke many things to them in parables, saying: "Behold, a sower went out to sow. "And as he sowed, some seed fell by the wayside; and the birds came and devoured them.

5. "Some fell on stony places, where they did not have much earth; and they immediately sprang up because they had no depth of earth. "But when the sun was up they were scorched, and because they had no root they withered away.

7. "And some fell among thorns, and the thorns sprang up and choked them. "But others fell on good ground and yielded a crop: some a hundredfold, some sixty, some thirty.
9. "He who has ears to hear, let him hear!"

***

Jesus Explains the Parable: (St. Matthew 13:18-23)

18. "Therefore hear the parable of the sower:
"When anyone hears the word of the kingdom, and does not understand it, then the wicked one comes and snatches away what was sown in his heart. This is he who received seed by the wayside.

20. "But he who received the seed on stony places, this is he who hears the word and immediately receives it with joy; "yet he has no root in himself, but endures only for a while. For when tribulation or persecution arises because of the word, immediately he stumbles.

22. "Now he who received seed among the thorns is he who hears the word, and the cares of this world and the deceitfulness of riches choke the word, and he becomes unfruitful.

23. "But he who received seed on the good ground is he who hears the word and understands it, who indeed bears fruit and produces: some a hundredfold, some sixty, some thirty."

Introduction Story

A business man took a taxi to the local airport...
Where he had rented a private plane...got out with briefcase in hand....

Saw a plane sitting on the runway warming up,
  Got in...
      Congratulated the pilot for being on time
          And they took off.

***

After gaining altitude the business man said...
    "This doesn't seem like the right direction for us to be going to Chicago".

The pilot said... "CHICAGO??? Why Chicago?
Business man: Well, that's where my meeting is...

After a moment of silence, the pilot said:
    "WHAT? You MEAN THAT YOU ARE NOT
        MY FLIGHT INSTRUCTOR???

***

Go... Sow Seeds

The scripture begins with Jesus going out to meditate by himself, but a large crowd of people ruined that, so he pushed off into a little boat and spoke to them from there.

Note: the pulpit of Cookeville CP Church is shaped like the prow of a boat.

Thoughts:

Jesus went to be alone and for prayer and meditation but of course there were **Interruptions**.

These interruptions are often an opportunity to
Share the gospel...JESUS DID!

JESUS WAS NOT A FARMER, but perhaps he looked to the fields and saw one sowing seeds and he used that occasion to teach a lesson that has transcended the centuries and has impacted the thoughts and lives of countless millions as we read, study, and try to comprehend everything that Jesus said and taught in this brief passage about the sowing of seeds in a field prepared to receive them.

Many things can happen when you try to sow seeds and most of them are ...
        NON-PRODUCTIVE, AND HARD WORK!

An un-answered question comes to mind as we search this scripture and await answers from the instruction that comes from prayer and study:

The question is: ARE SOME OF THESE SEEDS WASTED?

May I suggest four things that can happen which Jesus listed in this passage?

PRESUMPTION: that the farmer had already prepared the field for planting.

NOW LET ME SAY HERE...
    ...…that all those who have gone before you here in this church and in the work of God's Kingdom are the ones who have prepared your field for planting here.

Take a moment and think about them now...
        We sometimes call them the
        "GREAT CLOUD OF WITNESSES"

In a powerful moment of silence, let us pause to remember the ones who are no longer sitting in the places they always sat. Can't you hear the voice of some who led this congregation in prayer?

Do we presume that because they are no longer with us in body that they are not with us in spirit in this worship service, the very house of God?

The influence they imparted to us, and through us is not gone. Their voice, their commitment is surely in this place, the house of Almighty God.

***

Now look again to Jesus Parable
Which Jesus explained to the Disciples....?

NOTE: So far as I can think.... I do not remember that Jesus explained his other parables to them as he did this one.

Note:
We will look as the parable and to the explanation that Jesus gave. We will do this by examining what Jesus said using different translations of Holy Scripture. We will look at the different places where seeds fell and examine the analysis.

"And as he sowed, some seed fell (in the pathway), or by the Wayside... and the birds came and devoured them.

Note: Jesus explains the parable: Matthew 13:19 (RSV)
"When anyone hears the word of the kingdom, and does not understand it, then the wicked one comes and snatches away what was sown in his heart. This is he who received seed by the wayside".

These are people who hear the Gospel message but have a hardness of heart and won't listen...
    Know anyone like that?

Does this mean that these seeds are wasted?
Not at all!

Let me Illustrate:

We used to have this dog named Buster. Now Buster loved to run the back yard. He rarely escaped the back yard but he knew everything that went on in the front yard.

When anything happened in the front, or anyone walking in the road He

knew it. He would look through the fence on one side of the house...
    Then run to the other side of the house to see
    The front ...and he was fast.
    I called it Buster's 100 mile per hour pathway.
His continual running back and forth carved a deep pathway in our yard.
Buster died two years ago....
    And the grass seeds I planted over and over again
    On Buster's pathway are <u>just now</u> <u>covering</u> it
        up...

Perhaps you have planted some seeds in the lives of people you love and care for but they have turned a hardened heart to the Gospel... and to the Church.

Those seeds may yet come up...

REMEMBER... if the birds come and eat up the seeds, that ... BIRDS PLANT SEEDS TOO.

        ***

II

"Some fell on stony places, where they did not have much earth; and they immediately sprang up because they had no depth of earth.

And now here is the interpretation of the meaning of the Stone ground from the Living Bible, verse 20...

    The shallow, rocky soil represents the heart of a man   who hears the message and receives it with real joy, but he doesn't have much depth in his life, and the seeds   don't root very deeply, and after a while when trouble   comes, or persecution begins because of his beliefs, his
    enthusiasm fades, and he drops out.

Does this mean that these seeds are wasted?

Not at All........
    Remember we are people who have been born
    again and you just can't get unborn...

That person may fall away but we believe God will continue to call...
    God never forsakes us... Proverbs 22:6 reminds us that if we,

"...train up a child in the ways of the Lord and when he is old he will return to it...

***

III
"And some fell among thorns, and the thorns sprang up and choked them.

Verse 22 (Living Bible) says: The ground covered with thistles represents a man who hears the message, but the cares of this life and his longing for money choke out God's Word, and he does less and less for God.

Does this mean that these seeds are wasted?

No... These seeds are not wasted either, but they produce VERY LITTLE GRAIN, however, there may be a bit of hope for these seeds to be fruitful, some day.

<u>Again, let me try to illustrate...</u>

    Would you plant tomatoes among the thorns?
    Of course not.... But you know what? I Did!

Last year I planted tomatoes in an area that I had never tilled and I thought it; could become productive, even though it had nothing but weeds.

I killed the weeds (temporarily I found out later). And planted the tomato vines.
    I GOT A FEW TOMATOES,
        Some scratches and chiggers
        Trying to harvest them.
        SO I GAVE UP.

NOT LONG AGO, I WAS SPRAYING TO KILL THOSE WEEDS...
    And there was a Tomato vine with some green tomatoes on it
    AND I GOT SOME that were   planted last year.

And here is the explanation. This guy doesn't do much for God...BUT NOT WASTED.

***

IV

"But others fell on good ground and yielded a crop: some a hundredfold, some sixty, some thirty.

Living Bible Matthew, 13:23 says:
"The good ground represents the heart of a man who listens to the message and understands it and goes out and brings thirty, sixty, or even a hundred others into the Kingdom."

This one is self-explanatory and the one we attempt to emulate. It is the good seed, planted in good ground with no weeds to choke out the plants so that they grow and produce the good fruit of the kingdom, however, there is more.

Conclusion

We revert to the message in Matthew 13:9 which can be a confusing ending. It convicts us, no matter where we found ourselves in this parable, of not really listening to the power in this parable. It asks us if we are listening. So... we hear the convicting words found in...
Verse 9. "He who has ears to hear, let him hear!"

This really means... PAY ATTENTION!

It is time for the church to pay attention to what is happening around us and what is affecting the church adversely.

There is much concern in the evangelical church world today about the future of the church in North America.

A recent study uses the term "None's" who represent the young adults that are leaving the church in alarming numbers and are sometimes claiming no religion at all. Most developing trend lines are not encouraging. The percentage of Americans claiming no religion almost doubled in the past two decades, climbing from 8.1 percent in 1990 to 15 percent in 2008.

The trend isn't confined to one region. Those claiming no religion (aka Nones) made up the only group to have grown in every state, from the secular Northeast to the conservative Bible belt.

The Nones were most numerous among the young: a whopping 22 percent of 18- to 29-year-olds claimed no religion, up from 11 percent in 1990.

The study also found that 73 percent of Nones came from religious homes; 66 percent were described by the study as de converts.

Young adults are abandoning church at an alarming rate. It's interesting to ponder spiritual hunger and to look at these trends through the prism of the parable of the soils.

THIS IS OUR FIELD...Open to the Gospel

SO,
    We Love God
        Love His Church
            Love Children and we

    Certainly love each other in Christian
    Fellowship and service, then we are tilling the
        field and getting ready but now.... it is up to you to
        continue to...

GO PLANT SEEDS.....
    GOD WILL GIVE THE INCREASE.

In the name of Jesus Christ, our Lord...
AMEN!

Led by the Spirit

Acts 2:14-21

A friend of mine from high school days recently flew to California to visit his daughter. He told me this story, true? Not true? Who knows!

They touched down in Sacramento for a 45-minute lay over. Everyone left the plane except Gordon and a man sitting in front of him. My friend had noted the obedience and faithfulness of the seeing eye dog lying patiently on the floor, and that they were "regulars" on that flight, when the pilot came out of the cabin and said; "Hi Keith, want to get off and stretch your legs?" The man replied... "No, don't think so, but my dog needs a break"

PICTURE THIS...
 ....ALL those passengers who have just gotten off the plane are standing around in the gate area... then the pilot, wearing dark flight glasses walks off the plane with a SEEYING EYE DOG...
> AND NOBODY WANTS TO GET BACK
> ON THAT PLANE...

They don't know the history... They have a distorted picture...

To really be led by the Spirit is an awesome thing. To have the courage to be led by the spirit is a fearful thing... to be held in awe and reverence.

I BELIEVE
>   With all my heart
>>   That if the Cumberland Presbyterian
>>   Church is to have a meaningful future

WE MUST..... HAVE THE COURAGE
>   HAVE THE INSIGHT
>   AND RESPOND TO THE
>>   ILLUSIVE CALL TO

BE LED BY THE SPIRIT OF CHRIST

We would do well here to remember the theological concept of the Pneuma Cristi... the Spirit Christ, as we look to the Scripture. It is my belief that we have never had a real in-depth theology of the Holy Spirit, but then, it is a concept far beyond human comprehension.

Peter and the ten faithful Apostles were standing in Their NOW. They had just experienced the phenomena of God's Spirit being poured out on a gathering of thousands in an unexplainable way.

Peter, glanced into the past and declared the authenticity of the moment by proclaiming that they were not intoxicated, seeing that it was only 9:00 in the morning. THEY ARE NOT DRUNK, THEY ARE BEING LED BY THE SPIRIT. ALL OF THEM WERE.

PETER THEN MADE A PROCLAMATION ABOUT THE FUTURE.... (FROM THE PROPHET JOEL) Saying: "This is what will happen in the last days. God will pour out of his Spirit on everyone, on your Sons and Daughters,
And on Men and Women".

This theme became a watchword of the early church and was reiterated strongly in the Galatian passage (3:28) "..... There is no difference between Jews and Gentiles, slaves and free men, between men and women; you are all one in Christ Jesus...." (TEV)

I don't know where the church lost that, but thank God, we're seeing it restored in churches today, but I think someone forget to tell the Southern Baptist Convention about these Scriptures.

I live where there are many Native Americans. I grew up listening to their "SAGE SAYINGS". I was a white minority in a mostly Kiawa one-room country school. The Kiowa, among whom I was raised, were plains tribes, much different from our Choctaw, Cherokee and Chickasaw people where we have several congregations.

NOTE: The stole I often wear is written in the Cherokee (Tsa-la-gi) alphabet, a paraphrase of Matthew 11:28, "...his yoke is easy - his burden light". (It was made by Betty Booth Donohue and given to me because I was the last Moderator of Cherokee Presbytery before it merged into Red River Presbytery).

THE KIOWA had a saying.... (A philosophy of life that is reflective of the scripture we read). One of our family friends, Wesley Tappetoe who has long since departed this life, used to say:
    "I stand in the present
      I turn to the past and remember
        I walk bravely into the future".

How different from us that is. We most often start with History. They start with NOW... Like the Disciples.

Stand with me now, on a wind-swept hill on the vast open prairie. Look to your past, then turn your face to the wind and look to the future with hope.

WE ARE STANDING IN THE PRESENT

Can you imagine yourself standing alone, in the very presence of God, depending completely upon the reverence the past ...
    Process the past
        Understand the past
            Be thankful for our past..... And let it
                Guide us into our future...

...BUT EVERYONE HAS A PAST. My Cumberland Presbyterian Past is much different from yours, but we need to remember them together. As I tell you of my CP heritage I want you to remember yours.

I love the Cumberland Presbyterian Church. I probably cut my teeth on a church pew at Alden, Oklahoma, a church My Dad served as its organizing pastor.

NOTE: The Pulpit of the Alden Church has been donated to the Archives and holds the visitors book as you enter.

My Grandfather on my mother's side was the first CP elder we can find in our heritage. In 1906 Grandpa Trusty and My mother, age 10, made their way to the CP church in Midway Arkansas on a Sunday Morning in 1906. Mom was 10 years of age and remembered it clearly. They found a waiting congregation gathered outside the church. The doors were padlocked. After a while a representative from the "unionist" group came up, a Presbyterian Minister from Paris, AR who informed them that the church was a now Presbyterian Church, and that any of them wishing to worship as a newly organized congregation could follow him inside and begin Worship. According to Mom, after a few choice words from My Grandfather, they and the congregation adjourned to the brush arbor just across the way and held worship outside. The Minister and the organist he brought with him went inside....alone.

The church without a building floundered for a few Sundays, and then thankfully, the compassionate Southern Methodist church offered the

"Cumberlands" an arrangement where-by they could move into their building and have "Cumberland's preach on the first and third Sundays, Methodist would preach on the second and forth Sundays.

Six years later my Mother was married to Clint Scudder. The year was 1912. Five years after that, at the close of a Sunday morning service, a Methodist Sunday, under the powerful preaching of the visiting District Superintendent my dad responded to the call to the Gospel Ministry.

Mom and Dad quite often invited the ministers home for Sunday Dinner. The DS obliged. After a fine meal, I'm sure. (I can still remember Mom's Sunday Fried Chicken) They retired to the parlor where the DS proceeded to tell Dad exactly what steps he need to take to become a Methodist Minister. According to Mom Dad listened intently....
   Shaking his head with some approval,
      Asked several questions,

AND PROMPTLY BECAME, A CUMBERLAND PRESBYTERIAN. He and his younger brother, Houston Scrudder, cane under the care of Porter Presbytery near Ft. Smith, AR, and were both ordained together in 1919. In 1921 dad answered an ad in The Cumberland Presbyterian magazine, for ministers in the newly formed state of Oklahoma, and moved the family into Senator Oscar Lowrance's lake house at Lowrance Lake near Sulphur, OK. He was commissioned to organize congregations, mostly in school houses.
NOTE: (Oscar Lowrance was an Oklahoma State Senator with Cumberland Presbyterian heritage from West Tennessee.

About the Attempted Merger of 1906

AFTER THE attempted MERGER,
   THE CHURCH FLOUNDERED AND ALMOST DIED.
      BUT THE CHURCH REFUSED TO DIE. INSTEAD
      IT MOVED TO WHERE THE FRONTIER WAS....

THE WINDS OF CHANGE... winds of the Spirit, blew upon the church. My dad literally poured himself into preaching at established churches and organizing others. Some of them were: Tecumseh, Stratford, Alden, Mt Vernon, Rocky, and Cowden, all of which are long since passed, but think of the hundreds of people that found Christ through these short-lived churches.

THEN CAME WHAT I HAVE CHOSEN TO CALL THE THREE "D's" for Oklahoma, Draught, Dustbowl and Depression. The hot burning destructive winds of draught moved into Oklahoma and Texas… Oklahoma people still think all those three "D's" all came from Texas.

The Dust Bowl killed some churches. The migration away from the family farm to towns and cities after World War II killed THE others.

Some of the people struck oil during those hard times. Dad always maintained that it was easier to convert sinners to the Gospel during the Dust Bowl than it was just after they had struck oil.

THE PAST FOR THE CP CHURCH IS AWESOME

We are still standing on the very top of that hill, out there on the open plains where we can see in all directions. Off in this direction, I see my family and my own Story in the Cumberland Presbyterian Church. In This direction I see your story, your heritage, and if you look over here, you can almost see the Old Red River Meeting House from here. Just over there is the old log cabin of Samuel McAdow, and Old Beech Church over there. Many of those original Churches located near here are still serving.

THERE IS NEVER A DULL MOMENT WHEN YOU ARE BEING LED BY THE SPIRIT…

We stand here on the top of this hill and look in the distance and see the countless faithful witnesses who gave, and con-tine to give direction and guidance to us FROM THE PAST, INTO THE PRESENT, AND ON TO THE FUTURE.

I learned much more about this church when in 1954 I went to Bethel College, (now Bethel University). For the first time I realized that the WINDS OF THE SPIRIT were continuing to blow upon this fragmented church. I don't think most of us are willing to admit just how fragile,
    How fragmented
      How delicate
        The church was in those 40 years following the attempted union.

There were hurt feelings, and much anger and bitter resentment. The word "Presbyterian" was not a kindred name. It was more like a curse word. We were "Cumberlands" not Presbyterians!

After 40 years of wallowing in self-pity, after our 40 years in the wilderness, the Cumberland Presbyterian Church decided to take the sermonic advice of a sermon following the ill-fated merger, and "Live Again in the Sunlight of God's Love".

We started on a road to rebuild. Mission developments were started. Old resentments gave way..... Slowly, ever so slowly, even in my own family. In her last years my Mother actually belonged to A PCUSA Congregation. She, however, transferred her membership to Faith Church, Tulsa when I became pastor there so she could die a Cumberland Presbyterian and she did, though her funeral was in a PCUSA Church.

MANY DEDICATED LEADERS EMERGED, and gave sacrificially to lead us out of our wilderness... Some were: Arleigh Matlock, Morris Pepper, Harold Davis, Eugene Warren, and Carl Ramsey..... And there were others you will remember: Helen Deal, Beverly St. John, Virginia Malcolm and others... Many others!

MANY EXCELLENT PULPITEERS came to the front and carried the load... to build strong flag-ship congregations. Some were: Charles Zapp, J. Fred Johnson, E.K. Ragan, E.C. Cross, Burgis Cummingham, George Coleman and many others, built strong sizable congregations, but the winds of the Spirit blew upon them, and called them home. We have followed in their footsteps, so we know that THEIR WORKS ARE NOT GONE. Their evangelistic zeal accounts for thousands who still call Cumberland Presbyterian Theology their home and trace their religious experiences to those congregations....

THINK OF THE THOUSANDS OF PEOPLE
    Whose lives were changed.....?
    And were brought into the kingdom of God.

Remember! They were where God meant for them to be at that hour because they were being led by the Spirit.

MANY DEDICATED THEOLOGIANS, moved by the winds of the Spirit helped to re-form this church. People such as: Joe Ben Irby, E.K.

Regan, Hubert Morrow, Roy Blakeburn, Bob Shelton, and again, many others, many others!

COLLEGE AND SEMINARY PROFESSORS at the Cumberland Presbyterian Theological Seminary on Bethel Campus, such as: the Reverend, Doctor's, Virgil Todd, Colvin Baird, Bill Ingram, Joe Ben Irby, Hinkley Smartt, John Ed Gardner, Thomas Campbell… all gave themselves to educate several generations of the church. They became known as the Magnificent Seven.

Winds of the Spirit blew that Seminary right off the campus of Bethel College and into the metropolitan ministry of Memphis, TN where it serves a larger varied student body of many denominations of varied ethnic backgrounds, both Men and Women.

Early on the CP church struggled with issues of ordination of women, ordained many following the attempted merger. I remember especially some whose ministry were in Oklahoma such as: the Reverends, Mrs. Mable Reid, Mrs. Ada Slaton, and Mrs. DC Muphree. We also sent women as Missionaries. Berniece Barnett (Gonsoles) from Missouri and Ethel Brindle (Roa) from the Mt. Vernon Oklahoma congregation when my Dad, Reverend Clint Scrudder was pastor.

We stood our ground theologically in the midst of criticism from many segments of the body of Christ against such forward thoughts…
  But we have not practically
      Stood by our theology.
           We have not yet given ordained women
                Their rightful place…..

I am, however, convinced that the winds of the Spirit are still blowing upon us and that we are about to see once again, GOD MOVING THE CHURCH IN THE DIRECTION WE OUGHT TO GO TO FULFILL THAT PROPHETIC SCRIPTURE.

I am much encouraged by the winds of the Spirit as I see the spiritual development of YOUNG CUMBERLAND PRESBYTERIANS… Scores of our young people will spend hundreds of dollars to attend AND BECOME LEADERS in Triennium, CPYC and dozens of church camps where lives are still changed, and where they will grasp the calling that thrusts them into the wider church and into ministry.

YOUTH ADVISORY DELEGATES at general assembly will speak strongly within the committees where they serve and on the floor of the Assembly. They have made decisive differences on General Assembly Committees I have served on. They will go home and make a difference. Many of them will become church leaders, some Elders, some ordained ministers. Others will serve with dedication because of their religions experiences.
Youth and wisdom had spoken!

NOW WE MUST TURN FROM THE PAST AND LOOK TO AN UNCERTAIN FUTURE...

I am convinced, that out of all the issues that amount to a "hill of beans",
    The direction of the church, theologically,
        The ministries of the church to the world
            The outreach of the church into our
                Presbyteries and communities ...

...and reaching to all the PRESBYTERIES AND MISSION WORK The Cumberland Presbyterian Church, we will be what we are called to be, ONLY IF WE ARE LED BY THE SPIRIT.

Our beloved Church had it's real beginnings in sacramental camp meetings, and we will go stand on that holy ground as a part of this General Assembly, and we will pray for the leadership of the Spirit Christ to lead us into the future and, as long as God lets us serve. BUT WHO WILL LEAD US? GOD WILL PROVIDE!

                        ***

I have an awesome reverence for classical music, always have had. Such awesome talent! They weren't concerned about copyright, just about doing their best with what they had been given.

Some months ago I heard the sounds of a familiar Mozart concerto coming from my TV. (Oeta, the educational channel) but I like to crank it up and be surrounded with sound. The old TV just doesn't get it, but the music was strong, warm and rich...
        The director of the Orchestra was FLOWING
         With the music...from the piano.

The camera panned to the Piano, and I was shocked to see a frail little lady slumped over the keyboard. She was totally absorbed in her music. Nothing else mattered to her. She seemed to be alone with her music. The audience was not there. I did not see one sheet of music on the piano. She knew it all by heart...every note seemed to be perfect. And for the 37 minutes of that concerto her fingers moved in perfect concert with the full orchestra.

The camera zoomed in on her hands... and again I was shocked at what I saw. Every finger and joint was swollen, gnarled and twisted with Arthritis. I was glued to the TV... as I watched Alethia Dolorocha kept her audience spellbound as she effortlessly played through impossible cascading passages of that most difficult concerto.

At the conclusion her audience gave her a five-minute standing ovation.... but she had to be helped to rise from the piano and required help to leave the stage.

I AGONIZED... What a Talent! What a loss as she passes on to the end of her life and that talent is stilled and silenced forever...BUT HAVE ANY OF YOU SEEN THE CUTE LITTLE FIVE YEAR OLD GUY ON TV RECENTLY? (Whose name I have been unable to catch).

He just sat down at the piano and shocked his Mother as he began to play various classical pieces....! He had had no piano lessons, no training at all. The music came from his very being.

Now he reads the most difficult musical passages, will soon be on tour all over the United States, and he can also play Mozart's Piano Concerto # 27 by memory....

WOW... WHAT A GIFT! One talent passes on, another is born. Some congregations lived out their ministry and died out but others are born.

Church leaders live out their time... God sends others, but only if we are willing to be LED BY THE SPIRIT, and let our old men dream dreams, our young men see visions, and our women proclaim the wonderful gifts of god to all people.

WE ARE Proud to look to the past, but ever praying for the
LEADERSHIP OF THE SPIRIT CHIST,
    ....THE PNEUMA CHRISTI....

To lead us into TOMORROW,
AND EVEN INTO THE NEXT AGE...

WE ARE CHRISTIANS, standing in the NOW, remembering with thanksgiving our past, and stepping boldly with faith and hope into the future. AMEN!

Our Friend, the Church
Acts 11:19-26

The Church in Antioch

Now those who were scattered because of the persecution that took place over Stephen traveled as far as Phoenicia, Cyprus, and Antioch, and they spoke the word to no one except Jews.

But among them were some men of Cyprus and Cyrene who, on coming to Antioch, spoke to the Hellenists also, proclaiming the Lord Jesus.

The hand of the Lord was with them, and a great number became believers and turned to the Lord. News of this came to the ears of the church in Jerusalem, and they sent Barnabas to Antioch.

When he came and saw the grace of God, he rejoiced, and he exhorted them all to remain faithful to the Lord with steadfast devotion;

...for he was a good man, full of the Holy Spirit and of faith. And a great many people were brought to the Lord. Then Barnabas went to Tarsus to look for Saul, .and when he had found him, he brought him to Antioch.

So it was that for an entire year they met with the church and taught a great many people, and it was in Antioch that the disciples were first called "Christians."

Our scripture is a part of the stories of the Disciples....
    What they did, and
        Where they went this has always been enthralling to me.

It seems to me that we are walking in their footsteps and in order to do that we have to look at the footprints they made.

That journey started as a result of our scripture today.

REMEMBER......
    After the resurrection they were a bunch of
    Befuddled souls.

    Someone asked Daniel Boone if he had ever been lost, and he
    Replied... Nope... I've been befuddled for days at a time but I
    Have never been lost.

Those Disciples were a "Befuddled" bunch...
    Some to Emmaus
    Some went back to their nets...
        Where Jesus had challenged them
            - And sent them back to work.

That Mystery is cleared up for them
    AT THE ASCENSION
        Then the Great Commission, But...

BUT... you will be filled with the Holy Spirit, then you will be empowered to be my witnesses to:
    Jerusalem
        Judea and Samaria....
            And, to the ends of the earth.
  Then came Pentecost...

***

Our Scripture:

The Believers were scattered by the death and execution of Stephen

    <u>SO... Where did they go, what did they do?</u>

Some of them went to:
    Phoenicia...
        Cyprus...
            Antioch
But those preached to Jews Only.

SOME OF THE NEW CONVERTS WERE FROM
    CYPRUS AND CYRENE....
    (Could this have been Simon of Cyrene?????
    ...the one who carried Jesus' Cross? Some
    Say that it is, there is some Biblical proof),
    And now they are opening up a whole new field,
        That's us:
            ...THE GENTILES.

This News reached the church at Jerusalem....
    (James, in Charge)
        So they sent Barnabas to check it out...

Remember....
    This was their Commission...
        Go into all the world...and they finally did.

Barnabas found Paul and brought him to Antioch and they remained there for an entire year where they met with people of the church and formed a large congregation. It was here that they were first called CHRISTIANS.

They went to **form** churches everywhere... Some in homes, some in Jewish Synagogues...

    BUT IT WAS NEVER EASY.... AND IT IS NOT EASY NOW.
        AND...
    THEY WERE FIRST CALLED CHRISTIANS
        AT ANTIOCH

        ***

I SEE THE CHURCH OF TODAY...
    In every part of this event....

The Holy Spirit did come upon them and sent them into all the world with the Gospel message, which cost them their lives.

You see... the church has never had an easy time of it. Then or Now.

        ***

    Now I want to tell you a story

We have this friend (you and I)
    We love this friend.
        She is very old, and sometimes people tell us
        That she is at the point of death....

But we don't believe that.
>> She has been here a long time and,
>> She has lived in many countries...
>>> And lived thru good times and bad times...

> She has seen:
>> Poverty and Hatred
>> Wars and Anger
>> Division and Sickness

Thoughts:
> **Jesus Commissioned the Church**
>> **Don't just stand there, get with it.....**

***

<u>Our Friend, the Church</u>
<u>*Has made a lot of mistakes*</u>

Made a lot of enemies
> But has made millions of converts in every land
>> in every age...

The Church is in the midst of every War...to proclaim peace and Salvation.

She is in the midst of every Disaster... (Tornadoes or floods)

Our Friend...
> Has seen her sons and daughters slain by her enemies.
>> Has seen famine and pestilence ….......

This friend....
> Continually puts herself in danger.
>> Lives in dangerous neighborhoods...
>>> Won't stay out of trouble.

<u>Our Old Friend is Compassionate and Friendly...</u>

She loves people of every age...
> Every land
>> Every nation, race and ...

Welcomes strangers into her house...
...**Offers food and water** to all who enter...
EVEN TO THOSE WHO BREAK IN
AND STEAL THINGS. (And destroy the sanctity
Of our worship spaces)
<u>**She Loves her Enemies**</u>

***

SHE VISITS....
Homes where sickness and poverty are a way of life.
Loves homeless children and street people

SHE WALKS:
Lonely streets looking for hungry
Lost lonely children...

Walks Dark deserted Alleys, looking for
Derelicts and prostitutes.
WALKS...into the private lives of the WORLD

She is a Healer and she has **placed her hands:**
On the Sick
The Leper
The Outcasts of all societies...

On **Children** to BLESS
Missionaries to send them out into danger
Ministers to Preach...
And Elders to set them apart for special Work

On Soldiers who lay down their gun...
To give a child a stick of gum or candy bar

Yet....
She walks with Kings and Nobles
With Presidents and Paupers,
Even the Rich and Famous...
Love and serve Jesus Christ, our Lord
Because they came to know him through
Our friend, His Church.

***

Our Friend can be Hard to get along with

Especially when she became Angry.
    She Hates Sin: (But She Loves the Sinner).

She hates those who try to …
    Capitalize on people who are hurting,
    Those who try to trick people into believing,
    Hates Evil...
        And Evil-doers.

Hates Gossip....
    (Ever hear of the Gossip Ring???)

    Some European churches had one embedded in the brick just outside the doorway.

    Those caught in slanderous gossip...
        Were tied by the neck to that gossip ring
            And the congregation was supposed to
                Spit on them as they left services...
THAT' A LITTLE ROUGH...BUT,
    Our old friend hates gossip,

AND, hates those who say they come in the name of the Lord
But are not real ….

YET.... when she confronts a repentant sinner
    Her hatred is turned to love in one
        Swift Moment,
            Welcomes Sinners with Open Arms.

        Our Friend
Has many Sons and Daughters
Who try to convince her to take Her Rest...?

After All... She is very old and deserves a respite from her arduous labors ... After All, the world is filled with disease... She might catch a terminal disease...

They say:
>Stay out of the Marketplace... just live inside the closed varnished doors and the stained glass windows...
>Let the Church be the Church... and
>Let the world be the world...

***

She has Enemies...

Sometimes they paint graffiti on her doors
>And some of her enemies say... We hate the Cross
>>Keep that away from our Children
.   ..And out of the marketplace
We don't want to hear her voice in our streets.

But Remember...
>Jesus promised that the gates of Hell could **NEVER,** no Never
>>PREVAIL AGAINST THIS OLD FRIEND OF OURS.

As long as the world turns...
>And people live....
Our Friend the Church
>Will be knocking on the doors of Hearts,
>>**Calling Us to Serve...**
>>>Placing <u>our</u> hands on the work...
>>>>Ordaining people to go forth...Into the World, and remember,

WE were **first Called Christians at a place Called Antioch.**

AMEN!

Ashes, the Sign of the Cross
Matthew 26:36-41

36. Then Jesus came with them to a place called Gethsemane, and said to the disciples, "Sit here while I go and pray over there."

37. And He took with Him Peter and the two sons of Zebedee, and He began to be sorrowful and deeply distressed.

38. Then He said to them, "My soul is exceedingly sorrowful, even to death. Stay here and watch with me."

39. He went a little farther and fell on His face, and prayed, saying, "O My Father, if it is possible, let this cup pass from me; nevertheless, not as I will, but as you will."

40. Then He came to the disciples and found them asleep, and said to Peter, "What, could you not watch with me one hour?

41. "Watch and pray, lest you enter into temptation. The spirit indeed is willing, but the flesh is weak."

42. He went away again a second time and prayed, saying, "O My Father, if this cup cannot pass away from me unless I drink it, your will be done."

43. And He came and found them asleep again, for their eyes were heavy.

44. So He left them, went away again, and prayed the third time, saying the same words.

45. Then He came to His disciples and said to them, "Are you still sleeping and resting? Behold, the hour is at hand, and the Son of Man is being betrayed into the hands of sinners.

For 26 years, John Buchanan has pastored one of the most prestigious Presbyterian churches on the North American continent:

It was **Fourth Presbyterian Church** in Chicago, Illinois. Almost every service at which Dr. Buchanan presided, he began and closed each worship service with these words of beginning and benediction:

Startle us, O God, with your truth, and open our hearts and our minds to your word, that hearing, we may believe, and believing trust our lives, this day and all the days that lie ahead, to your love. In Jesus Christ our Lord. Amen.

***

SEEMS TO ME THAT WE ARE NO LONGER STARTLED BY THE CROSS

No matter what you thought about Mel Gibson's interpretation of **The Crucifixion of Christ** ....We were startled by how horrible it was. We simply cannot fathom the horrible torture that this kind of execution inflicted on the one condemned to die. It is also beyond our comprehension that people loved to see this kind of execution. We know that they gathered to watch and participate.

I wonder what happened to the Cross.

I Mean, the old rugged cross? The actual cross on which Jesus died...
AFTERWARDS...Did they lay it on the ground and pull out the nails and make it ready for the next victim?

Was **The Cross** waiting for another man to be nailed to its arms and be lifted back up to kill another person?

COULD IT BE........?

Could it be that some of the followers of Jesus got hold of it and reserved it? NO... THAT WOULD BE A BIT ABSURED TO THINK THAT....

They really had no idea at the time that the cross would take on any leaning for them except a hated instrument of execution of their blessed lord, JESUS CHRIST.

YET...

> YET, WE HAVE THAT CROSS WITH US TONIGHT.
> THAT CROSS HAS BEEN PRESERVED FOR **ALL**
> WHO BELIEVE..... (And the world hates it)
>
> They don't want it in public places... not around your necks...
> OR ON YOUR DESK AT WORK. It is a constant reminder to the non-believer of the commitment it alludes to when one will wear that cross.

The Ashes we shall use tonight will be the sign of the cross marked upon your forehead.

Like wearing the cross around our necks, the wearing of the ashes will be cause for people to question you, or even ridicule you for doing such a silly thing, and especially if you have the courage to wear it tonight as you leave or even tomorrow as you go back to your usual routine.

(MANY WOULD LAUGH AT YOU FOR DOING SUCH A SILLY THING)...

>HOW NAIVE OF US
>   TO THINK WE CAN MAKE
>   A SACRIFICE LIKE THAT

But we are not the sacrifice. Jesus was (IS) our sacrifice. The Ashes are supposed to make us aware of our commitment to the one who was sacrificed on that horrible cross and it is our testimony that He did it for every one of us.

***

THE SEASON OF LENT CALLS US TO LOOK AT <u>THE WAY OF THE CROSS</u>

By using the term (way of the cross) we reflect on the **Pathway of the Cross.**

That pathway was the pathway that Jesus walked with the disciples for three years. Everywhere he and they went Jesus told them, and reminded them that it was a pathway leading to Jerusalem and finally to the Jerusalem that would crucify Him.

<u>The Sacrifice of Jesus</u>

Started at his Baptism and immediately it continued as he was driven into the wilderness to be tempted by Satan. That Sacrifice for you and me continued for the three years of his earthly ministry.

Even the disciples who committed themselves to follow Jesus made some sacrifices. Surely they all had families they left behind. Surely they had other plans, some fishermen, and there was even a tax collector among them.

The pathway took Jesus and the disciples across the borders into the territory of Samaria.

It took them into personal contact with diseased lepers who were the lowest of outcast in their society.

It took them into homes that were friendly like Mary, Martha and Lazarus, or into the homes of Pharisees where most of them were hostile toward Jesus. Finally it took them back to Jerusalem and into the upper room where they were prepared for the supreme sacrifice that Jesus would make, but they were lulled into non-belief.

This horrible think just could not be thrust upon Jesus and certainly not to each of them.

The supper in the upper room was a powerful and wonderful thing but that wonderful experience just wouldn't last.

As they left singing one of their favorite hymns they entered the garden of prayer where some of them would take their rest while Jesus anguished in prayer and where Jesus would...

Turn himself completely over to his Father, Almighty God. He would be arrested and then be taken to the home

CIAIPHAS, then on to the hall of Pilate early the next morning where he would be condemned in a false mock trial.

AND FINALLY.... that terrible scene on the hill of Golgotha where that sacrifice became the most terrible DEATH imaginable

THUS

WE START ON OUR PATHWAY
OF 40 DAYS OF PREPARATION
FOR EASTER MORNING and the
Resurrection of Jesus Christ, our Lord.

***

When I think of this long pathway toward the cross I cannot remove a picture I remember from my childhood at old Mt. Vernon Cumberland Presbyterian Church, near Mt. View, Oklahoma. I must not have been more than six or seven years old. My Dad was preaching. I remember looking toward a wall near the pew where I was sitting. I saw a Picture that stuck in my childhood mind... Not pretty, roughly painted, the picture was of a cone-shaped hill with a pathway leading to the top with a cross on the top.

I remember some of the words of the old gospel song that evidently inspired that "work of art". **The words** went something like this:

> I must needs go home by the way of the cross.
> There's no other way but this.
> As I onward go it is sweet to know,
> The way of the cross leads home.

Truly, the pathway (the way) of that old rugged cross leads us to our eternal home and it is a reminder that we are called to be like him and as we wear these ashes we remember that we are not ashamed to wear the sign of repentance proudly.

NOTE: On Palm Sunday the palm branches are often made into the shape of the cross... then after they turn brown and die. That small cross is set on fire and burned giving us the ashes to be used next year.

***

I love the hymn..."Lift High the Cross"

It is our closing Hymn and will lead us to come to the kneeling rail for the affixing of the sign of the cross on our foreheads.

Before we sing it think about the words and see the liturgy that could be so symbolic. In your minds see the Acolytes enter the sanctuary with the Light of Christ, and then see them bringing in the Holy Scriptures.

Now add to that the cross and the one carrying in that cross lifting it high as the congregation joins in singing those powerful words. All of the verses have powerful messages but the refrain ties them together with these words...

"Lift High the Cross, the love of Christ proclaim, 'til all the world adores his wonderful name".

Tonight as we come and kneel at this kneeling rail for prayer and acknowledgment of the ashes and the cross let us depart in peace and re-enter the world with that sign of the cross on our brow but most of all....

IN OUR HEARTS...Amen!

What Happens Next?
Luke 8; Matthew 13

4. And when a great crowd came together and people from town after town came to him, he said in a parable:

5. "A sower went out to sow his seed; and as he sowed, some fell along the path, and was trodden under foot, and the birds of the air devoured it.

6. And some fell on the rock; and as it grew up, it withered away, because it had no moisture.

7. And some fell among thorns; and the thorns grew with it and choked it.

8. And some fell into good soil and grew, and yielded a hundredfold." As he said this, he called out, "He who has ears to hear, let him hear."

9. And when his disciples asked him what this parable meant,

10. He said, "To you it has been given to know the secrets of the kingdom of God; but for others they are in parables, so that seeing they may not see, and hearing they may not understand.

Matthew 13:

33. Another parable He spoke to them: "The kingdom of heaven is like leaven, which a woman took and hid in three measures of meal till it was all leavened."

34. All these things Jesus spoke to the multitude in parables; and without a parable He did not speak to them,

35. That it might be fulfilled which was spoken by the prophet, saying: "I will open my mouth in parables; I will utter things which have been kept secret from the foundation of the world."

I believe most all of you have been a story teller at one time or another...or perhaps you have been a listener to someone telling those stories.

>Sometimes the stories are true
>Sometimes they are fairy tales without a bit of truth in
>them ....

All kinds of Stories...
>About your childhood... things you did... funny things   you said.
>>About our culture
>>>Native Americans told their history in stories.

My mother made up stories that would scare the living daylights out of you…
Well, we hoped they were made-up stories.

There are now even national Story-Telling Events with big prizes for the person who can tell the biggest tale…
    (I suppose that on is usually won by someone from Texas)

MOTHERS are always able to tell when their children are "telling stories", you know, instead of telling the truth.

In case the story teller runs out of time and has to stop before the story is ended…. The listeners (usually trying to keep from going to bed) say… YOU CAN'T QUIT NOW…WHAT'S NEXT?

                      ***

JESUS WAS A STORY -TELLER…

His stories carried VIVID PICTURES
                BOLD IMMAGERY
                    POWERFUL EMAGINATIONS
            SOME WERE EVEN HUMUROUS

How about:
    A fence post compared to a speck ….Luke 6:41
    Why do you see the speck that is in your brother's eye,
        but do not notice the log that is in your own eye?

Luke 10: 48-49. Jesus speaks of those who hear his words
        but will not do what he teaches…

48. He is like a man building a house, who dug deep, and laid the foundation upon rock; and when a flood arose, the stream broke against that house, and could not shake it, because it had been well built.
49. But he who hears and does not do them is like a man who built a house on the ground without a foundation; against which the stream broke, and immediately it fell, and the ruin of that house was great."

AND THEY COULDN'T WAIT TO REBUILD NEW ORLEANS, BELOW SEA – LEVEL.

Have they not read this story about the Wise man and the foolish man building upon the solid rock, or on the shifting sand?

What different outcome do they expect the next time? And it will most likely happen again, may be many years later but it will happen again.

***

DO WE GET THE PICTURE? Are we understanding why??? Why Jesus told all of these parables and then had to explain some of them to his Disciples who had very little imagination?

It is very clear to us that Jesus spoke so the hecklers wouldn't understand and the Disciples…would get it. The messages were "ENCRIPTED"!

***

Do you know the Stories of Jesus?

I found 35 stories Jesus told as Parables and that may not be all of them. If you have read your bibles

> If you have been in SS classes
> And Bible Studies….

. . .you probably do know all of them, but since we are also "disciples" perhaps we have not dug deeply enough into them to completely understand some of those "encrypted" thoughts that come to us when we, "open the book and open out minds to receive the things that apply most to our lives and our situations.

I could ask you and you could remember many of those parables, may be not correctly… or perhaps our
> Interpretation is skewed a bit,
>> But we know the stories of Jesus.

Jesus told stories about:
> An enemy planting bad seeds in a field…
>> Mustard Seed
>>> Seeds of every kind

> Weeds in a good crop of wheat

About:
> A pearl of great price
>> A treasure hid in a field
>>> Rich man and Lazarus
>>>> A man refusing to help his neighbor,
>>>> Who had un-expected company...

About:
> Bringing a child to him as he said....

"Except you become as a little child you cannot enter the Kingdom of Heaven..."

Or about a wedding banquet
> A Wayward Son
>> A Lost Coin
>>> A Lost Sheep.

And all of those powerful Parables are really about the Kingdom of God and about Jesus Himself...

Perhaps all of you will remember the most powerful one (even though we did not read that scripture, you probably know it by heart) It is about the owner of the vineyard. Which of course the Pharisees understood to be God, and about those renters (the Jews) who had killed many prophets, and now were about to murder God's own Son, Jesus himself.

Wow! This is Jesus fore-telling what the Pharisees were planning to do to him. I'm not sure the Disciples got it but the Pharisees got that one. It hit them in their very being but it didn't change them. It just infuriated them and they became even more determined to make this one come true by continuing to plain the death of Jesus.

Now, getting back to our story...

II

Do YOU live by, and tell the Stories of Jesus?

***

Some of you will remember with fondness the powerful old song written by Fanny Crosby, Tell me the Story of Jesus.

(It has three verses and all of them tell in sequence, parts of the life stories of Jesus)

>Tell Me the Story of Jesus,
>>Write on my heart every word.
>
>Tell me the story most precious,
>>Sweetest that ever was heard.
>
>Tell How the Angels in Chorus
>>Sang as thy welcomed his birth.
>
>Glory to God in the highest!
>>Peace, and good tidings to earth.

>Fasting alone in the Desert,
>>Tell of the days that are past.
>
>How for our sins he was tempted
>>Yet was triumphant at last.
>
>Tell of the years of his labour,
>>Tell of the sorrow he bore.
>
>He was despised and afflicted,
>>Homeless, rejected and poor,

>Tell of the Cross where they nailed Him
>>Writhing in Anguish and Pain,
>
>Tell of the grave where they laid Him
>>Tell how he loveth again.

(And perhaps the most message of all is the ending of verse, which says)...
Love in that story most tender
>Clearer than ever I see,
>>Stay, Let me weep while you whisper

LOVE PAID THE RANSOM FOR ME.

YES… Someone told you the story of Jesus and now it is placed upon your heart to tell that Story of Jesus, so that it may be written on someone else's heart.

But you also have a story about how you met Jesus and how you are to share it by the way you live your life. So ask yourself, what is the most powerful part of my relationship with Jesus Christ, our Lord?

III

DO YOU HAVE A STORY TO TELL?
 YES! YOU DO! AND YOU NEED TO TELL IT

***

When did you first meet Jesus?
What is your witness?
When did you first know that Jesus?

WHAT DOES JESUS MEAN TO YOU?

What has Jesus done for you?

Go, tell the Stories of Jesus and tell your story, that is,
What you are doing for Him?

AND, have you told your children?
Your Grand Children…
Your Great Grandchildren?

Have you told your neighbor who does not go to church…? Or may be does not even know about Jesus

Jesus is the real Gospel and the Gospel is about the
REAL JESUS…

***

IV

DOES YOUR CHURCH HAVE A STORY TO TELL?

(Yes! It Does! And each of you need to be a part of how this church conveys the Love of Jesus Christ to this community,
And to the world).

(WITNESS TO THE COMMUNITY)

Tell the story of your church! This story is about a Church starting on the Frontier that loved Jesus more than anything, and how that frontier church grew out of great preaching, and revivals.

Tell how the Cumberland Presbyterian Churches in this area
      Love Jesus Christ as Lord and How WE ARE following the BOOK (the Bible).

Tell How, it has reached out to People with the Salvation
      That only Jesus can give...

Conclusion:

Jesus told a lot of stories about SEEDS...
      Mustard Seed...
           Planting good seeds

When I was quiet young, perhaps seven or eight... Dad bought a big watermelon... it was HUGE... and we cut it. It was as red as could be and of course we had to eat it all. (No refrigeration)

Boy that thing was good... (Almost as good as the one that Con gave us that brought $600.00 at the Water-melon Festival).

Dad said: "Umm Umm... that's the best watermelon I've ever tasted... Son, save those seeds", and saved every one of them. The next spring I planted every one of them in good sandy soil and I carried water to all of those hills on hot days when we had no rain the vines grew, the melons came on them and grew, but not as big as that one Dad bought finally we decided to cut one. It was hard as a rock but I finally got it cut, almost had to "bust it open"

Anybody out there ever heard of a PIE MELON?

I DON'T KNOW WHAT THEY REALLY ARE….but I know they are not fit to eat….

Be careful what you plant.
If you sow good seeds they will grow in the hearts and lives of people.

GO! PLANT GOOD SEEDS! And the good seeds, planted in the hearts and lives of the people you know will grow, perhaps not immediately but when we plant good seeds of the stories of Jesus those seeds will someday come up and bear fruit.

AND THE STORY OF THE KINGDOM GOES ON…
LET'S SEE WHAT HAPPENS NEXT IN THIS CHURCH AND THE CHURCHES IN THIS AREA…

And the kingdom of God will continue to grow here

May God richly bless your planting?

Pastor: Amen!
People: And Amen

Courage to Live by Faith
(Live by Love)
(Mother's Day Sermon)
1 Corinthians 13 (NIV)

1. If I speak in the tongues of men and of angels, but have not love, I am only a resounding gong or a clanging cymbal.
2. If I have the gift of prophecy and can fathom all mysteries and all knowledge, and if I have a faith that can move mountains, but have not love, I am nothing.
3. If I give all I possess to the poor and surrender my body to the flames, but have not love, I gain nothing.
4. Love is patient, love is kind. It does not envy, it does not boast, it is not proud.
5. It is not rude, it is not self-seeking, it is not easily angered, and it keeps no record of wrongs.
6. Love does not delight in evil but rejoices with the truth.
7. It always protects, always trusts, always hopes, and always perseveres.
8. Love never fails. But where there are prophecies, they will cease; where there are tongues, they will be stilled; where there is knowledge, it will pass away.
9. For we know in part and we prophesy in part,
10. But when perfection comes, the imperfect disappears.
11. When I was a child, I talked like a child, I thought like a child, I reasoned like a child. When I became a man, I put childish ways behind me.
12. Now we see but a poor reflection as in a mirror; then we shall see face to face. Now I know in part; then I shall know fully, even as I am fully known.
13. And now these three remain: faith, hope and love. But the greatest of these is love.

John 19:23-27 (RSV)

23. When the soldiers had crucified Jesus they took his garments and made four parts, one for each soldier; also his tunic. But the tunic was without seam, woven from top to bottom;
24. So they said to one another, "Let us not tear it, but cast lots for it to see whose it shall be." This was to fulfil the scripture, "They parted my garments among them, and for my clothing they cast lots."
25. So the soldiers did this. But standing by the cross of Jesus were his mother, and his mother's sister, Mary the wife of Cleopas, and Mary Magdalene.
26. When Jesus saw his mother, and the disciple whom he loved standing near, he said to his mother, "Woman, behold, your son!"

27. Then he said to the disciple, "Behold, your mother!" And from that hour the disciple took her to his own home.

I believe this is a time for those of the Faith to live the faith.

The greatest attribute of the "Faithful" is to:
    Live like Jesus lived
    To love as he loved
    And to be found faithful to our calling.

I Cor 13: is one of the most powerful chapters in the bible… because it challenges us to do just that…
  It is a perfect way to emphasize the spread of   the teachings of Jesus and to…
    CAPTURE THE ESSENCE OF
        MOTHERHOOD… (Parenthood)

This is pick on Mom's day, you know…
    A day when you are HONORED
        And ADMONISHED, all at the same time….
            Let me say just a word about that.

Mothers and Grandmothers….
………have been known to scold little boys for carrying
    Such yucky things in their pockets, Things Like:
        Frogs and remains of a peanut and Jelly sandwich,
        (All in the same pocket)
            Marbles and Rocks, Rubber bands and toy Cars…
            and fishing worms and ….all the other things they have been known to carry…

Before scolding them too severely, YOU Mothers and Grandmothers might need think for a moment of all the things YOU ARE CARRYING
    AROUND IN YOUR PURSES….
        (Not going there)…

NOTE: A wonderful Grandmother of the New Ebenezer Church in West Tennessee was just such a person. All the kids in the church wanted to sit with MISS MEXIE…

Because they couldn't ask for something she didn't have in her B-I-G PURSE...

ENOUGH OF THAT...

ANYWAY MOMS (and Grand-mons).... YOU ARE THEIR   EXAMPLE...

I CORINTHIANS 13 TEACHES

We may be eloquent and attain much in this life but if we do not exemplify love of Christ.... We are nothing.
 Love is all the things listed there:
  Patient, Kind,
   Not Ill-mannered or selfish, nor irritable.

Paul says: I could even sacrifice myself... but if I do not have love I am nothing...

Inspired Message are temporary (sermons)
  Tongues shall all pass away
    Everything we say will pass away
      Everything we do will pass away,

BUT ...LOVE IS ETERNAL....

AND IT GIVES US THE COURAGE TO LIVE BY FAITH...i.e. by love.

SO......... HOW DO WE DO THAT?
  HOW DO WE LIVE THE FAITH?

I

FIRST….. LET US KNOW THAT THE FAITHLESS HAVE NO RESOURSES TO DRAW FROM….

A few years ago…while doing an Interim at Brenthaven in Nashville, we were grabbing a bite in a fast-food place.
    I struck up a conversation with a kid who was moping the floors in this fast-food place. (We were the only ones in the dining area)…

In a few minutes we knew a lot more about him than perhaps we wanted to know, for truly this kid had the gift of gab.

WE LEARNED…
    That he was tired.
        That he was 26 years old and expecting his first
      Child.
          That he was working three jobs
            That he was saving his money to go to
An S-U-P-E-R PARTY IN New Orleans

Then ……..he was going (to hook up) with some friends….
    To PARTY IN AMSTERDAM….
And…..

    Had refused to take his EXPECTANT WIFE WITH HIM…

His philosophy…. "LIFE IS A PARTY YOU ONLY LIVE ONCE…
    HE HAS NOTHING TO DRAW ON…
    HIS WELL IS EMPTY.

Any of you out there remember how it is to

        DRAW WATER FROM A WELL….?

I have, and if you ever did that you had hope as you lowered that bucket on a rope that the bucket and the rope would stay intact but your main hope was that there was good fresh water in that old well.

Jesus is the refreshing water that feeds out thirsty lives.

II

THE FAITHFUL ARE SUSTAINED BY THE HAND OF GOD.
  …...God is Love....

Life is full of hard choices…
  …......and we make those choices in the context of our faith.
  ….…..OR THE LACK OF IT….…..

Some of those choices have UN - intended consequences...

  YOU KNOW THAT THIS CHURCH HAD MADE
      SOME OF THOSE HARD CHOICES THAT THERE ARE
          SOMETIMES UN-INTENDED CONSEQUINCES....

(We all have done that)

GO WITH ME TO THE CROSS NOW…
      (And remember the Scripture of the morning, with Mary
          and others standing near the cross)

Mary stood there watching her young son die.
      She made a hard choice.….a choice to be there.
      What else could she do?
  It was a "MOTHERHOOD" KIND OF CHOICE....

NO! SHE DIDN'T WANT TO BE THERE …
      But she was held there ...as strongly as the nails held
          Her Son to that horrible cross.
              (No pride here…. Only pain and love)

She couldn't say: LOOK THAT'S MY SON UP THERE
          RECEIVING ALL THOSE HONORS…
              She could only weep and say… THAT"S My Son…
                  TRULY HER LOVE WAS CORAGEOUS

TO BRING CHILDREN INTO THE WORLD TODAY IS TRULY
COURAGEOUS…. (Truly an act of faith).

  MOTHERHOOD/ PARENTHOOD
      IS AN INVESTMENT

A CHALLENGE
A FRIGHTENING THING....

WE MUST RISK EVERYTHING ON THIS ...
.....INVESTMENT.

Soon .....We'll move on down the hallways of time and we'll pass and be forgotten like the rest....

Cartoon:

Dennis .... In a rare reflective moment,
   Says to his Mom, whom he adores......

 (And is probably thinking of Margaret whom he
  Cannot stand)...

HE SAYS: Mom... "Were you pretty when you were a
   Little girl...OR, did you just get that way
   ….......when you got old?

Finally we ask....

III

HOW DO WE HAVE COURAGE TO
      LIVE THE FAITH? BY LOVE
            WHEN THE INVESTMENT GOES BAD...

Our world...
        ...and perhaps our churches,
              Have failed the test to show young people how to live in
              the context of faith.

REAL PARENTHOOD TEACHES, AND LIVES BY,
   THE PRINCIPLES OF I CORINTHIANS 13.

SOMEHOW…. Somehow, I believe as Paul penned these lines to the
    Corinthian Christians he was thinking of Jesus as he died on the
    cross…Jesus loved even those who nailed him to the cross.

THEN WE SEE MARY… standing there looking at her Son.
  She never gave up on him….
  We don't give up on ours either

***

NOW LET ME SPEAK A WORD ABOUT THE
CHURCH WE NEVER GIVE UP……

Do you love this church?
   (Obviously you do or you wouldn't be here...)

Do you love this community? Yes...

Are you concerned for the young people here?
      (You know we are)

Do you want this witness to Jesus Christ our Lord?
To continue here?
       (Of course we do)...

This church has been Mother, Father, and Parent
       To countless numbers of people....

DO NOT LET THE VISION DIE...
       REACH DOWN DEEP ….
              AND...
                     PROCLAIM THE LOVE OF JESUS
                            CHRIST OUR LORD...

There are countless numbers of people out there
Who are in desperate need of that love...?

AND YOU CAN GIVE IT.

***

STAND WITH MARY…
        BUT HEAR THE WORDS OF I COR…13

        LOVE HAS MANY LANGUAGES…

If I have not love I am nothing
        I may be wealthy or poor… but if I do not have
            Love… I am nothing…

LOVE DOES NOT COUNT WRONGS
        NEVER GIVES UP… never ends….

WE HAVE FAITH HOPE AND LOVE….
        BUT THE GREATEST OF THESE IS LOVE.

        In the name of Father, Son, and Holy Spirit!
        AMEN!

Light from the Mountain
Luke 9: 28-42

After saying these things, about eight days later, Jesus took Peter, James, and John and went up on top of a mountain to pray.

While Jesus was praying, his appearance began to change. His clothes became as bright as a flash of lightning. Suddenly, two men were talking with Jesus. They were Moses and Elijah.

Moses and Elijah were shining brightly, too. They were talking with Jesus about his death which was about to be fulfilled in Jerusalem.

Peter and the others were deep in sleep, but they woke up and saw the glory of Jesus. They also saw the two men who were standing with Jesus.

As Moses and Elijah were about to leave, Peter said, ``Teacher, it is good that we are here. We will set up three holy tents--one for you, one for Moses, and one for Elijah." (Peter didn't know what he was saying.)

While Peter was saying these things, a cloud came all around them. Peter, James, and John became afraid when the cloud covered them.

A Voice came from the cloud, saying, ``this is My Son; he is my chosen one. Listen to what he says!" When the Voice finished, only Jesus was there. Peter, James, and John said nothing. At that time, they told no one about what they had seen.

The next day they came down from the mountain. A large group of people met Jesus. A man from the crowd cried out to Jesus, ``Teacher, please come and look at my son. He is the only child I have.

A spirit gets hold of my son, and suddenly he shouts. He loses control of himself and he foams at the mouth. It hurts him and it will almost never leave him.

I begged your followers to make it leave him, but they were not able to." Jesus answered, ``you people are a generation with no faith. You are warped. How long must I be with you and put up with you?"

Then Jesus said to the man, ``Bring your son here." While the boy was coming, the demon threw him on the ground. The boy lost control of himself. Jesus gave *a command to the evil spirit and healed the boy. Then Jesus gave him back to his father.*

Prayer for Enlightenment: (from ancient liturgies)

>Come Holy Spirit…
>>Come as the Wind and cleanse
>>>Come as the Fire and Burn
>>>>Come as the Light and Reveal

Convict, Convert, Consecrate until we are wholly yours…

Churches and individuals are both called to do ministry. In order to do that we must spend time alone with God. Individuals experience the call to ministry and thus, need to spend prayerful time in preparation.

Churches call pastors they hope will lead them into deeper commitment and expanded ministry. In order for churches to do that the church leaders need to spend prayerful time in extending the call to a pastor.

SO………..WHAT IS THE CALL? The Call is two-fold:

Dr. Bill Ingram, Memphis Theological Seminary, who taught me and probably some who will read this sermon, said:

>"You must have two calls to be a pastor"
>>The first call is from God,

Note:
I believe that God's call has brought churches and individuals together so that they may both answer the calling together. It takes prayer and enlightenment for a church to call a pastor and it takes prayerful consideration for a pastor to respond to the calling of a congregation that extends the call. It is no little thing to step into the sacred pulpit and serve this church.

Then the person responding to the call of Almighty God, must have a call from a church that believes in them and will promise to support that person in the God-called ministry.

Well…, there are other ways, of course. Persons don't have to have a call from a church if that individual wants to stand on a street corner and button whole people to try to tell them about the Gospel… But Church is better equipped to enable ministry to homeless, and, or, street corner preaching. We do need to get out on the street corners.

The Call is from God:
>That call never goes away
>>It may change from place to place
>>From time to time
>>>From one kind of ministry to another
>>>>But…It never goes away.

The call from a church can, and often does, go away.
That call can go away and be dissolved by common agreement,
Or, pastors can be fired like people in the outside world.

We have talked about the calling of individuals and of churches seeking to expand their ministry so let us return to the thoughts that come to us from our scriptural passage and let those words guide us in a spiritual way.

Now let us look deeply into our Scripture:

Jesus had taken His Inner-circle Disciples up to a high mountain. In Israel, it may have been sort of like this high place. We do not know whether it was Mt. Hermon which was the highest in the region, or Mt, Tabor which was a two day walk from Nazareth.

It is great to be on the Mountain with Jesus

Peter, James, and John and went up on top of a mountain to pray. While Jesus was praying, his appearance began to change. His clothes became as bright as a flash of lightning.

Suddenly, two men were talking with Jesus. They were Moses and Elijah. Luke 9:31 Moses and Elijah were shining brightly, too. They were talking with Jesus about his death which was about to be fulfilled in Jerusalem.
32. Peter and the others were deep in sleep, but they woke up and saw the glory of Jesus. They also saw the two men who were standing with Jesus.
LET'S JUST STAY HERE

As Moses and Elijah were about to leave, Peter said, ``Teacher, it is good that we are here. We will set up three holy tents--one for you, one for Moses, and one for Elijah." (Peter didn't know what he was saying.)

34. While Peter was saying these things, a cloud came all around them. Peter, James, and John became afraid when the cloud covered them.

35. A Voice came from the cloud, saying, ``this is My Son; he is my chosen one. Listen to what he says!"

36. When the Voice finished, only Jesus was there. Peter, James, and John said nothing. At that time, they told no one about what they had seen.

We are well aware of the term, Mountain-top-experience. Many of us have had such experiences and would surely like to capture those times and keep them alive, but we often have to return to the valley where there is heartbreak and trouble.

It was Simon Peter who wanted to stay on the mountain top and build three holy places but Jesus denied that request.

Note: The early church fathers evidently believed that the mountain of Transfiguration was Mt. Tabor. Shortly after Rome legalized Christianity, by the early 400's they build the Church of the Transfiguration atop Mt. Tabor.

Trouble in the Valley

Jesus would not let them stay on the mountaintop. The next day, they returned to the valley where they encountered the other Disciples in the midst of a troubled crowd. They were attempting to do ministry but had failed miserably.

Verses 37-ff. The next day they came down from the mountain. A large group of people met Jesus. A man from the crowd cried out to Jesus, ``Teacher, please come and look at my son. He is the only child I have. An evil spirit gets hold of my son, and suddenly he shouts. He loses control of himself and he foams at the mouth. It hurts him and it will almost never leave him. I begged your followers to make it leave him, but they were not able to."

SO..........What are we to do?
Verse 41: Jesus answered, ``you people are a generation with no faith. You are warped. How long must I be with you and put up with you?" Then Jesus said to the man, ``Bring your son here."

42.   While the boy was coming, the demon threw him on the ground. The boy lost control of himself. Jesus gave a command to the evil spirit and healed the boy. Then Jesus gave him back to his father.

***

Get Off the Mountain

Jesus was obviously disgusted with what was happening with his disciples who were not able to help the young man and his Father who were in great trouble. Jesus took control and restored the young man immediately.

Let us speak frankly about this need to get ourselves off the mountain and outside the Church for ministry. We use this passage to take a close look at ourselves and see that we would rather stay at the church than to return to our troubled neighborhoods. Worship can be our mountaintop.

Anyone who has ever climbed a mountain knows that it is easier going up than coming down, even if it is a small mountain like the ones I climbed as a teenager in Southwest Oklahoma.

Even though those Wichita Mountains are small one can see great distances from the top. One can drive a spiraling paved road to the top of Mt. Scott but if you want a better distant vision you must climb the hard way to the top of Mt. Sheridan. Once you have done that you want to stay there awhile but there is nothing atop that mountain. No water, no food… nothing, so you don't want to stay there very long. Then you find that coming down it hard, tricky and very dangerous.

(Mt Scott)

Mt. Scott It is only 2,500 ft. high with a cork-screw kind of road winding to the top… very near to Mt. Sheridan. I have loved to visit that mountain most of my life. For a flatlander, the drive up that spiraling road with no guard rails, only boulders to keep you from dropping hundreds of feet, will scare you to death.

Some wild teenagers that I knew very well used to play a game of putting their car into high gear, when cars had only standard shift transmissions, and would start down the mountain from the very top, pledging not to touch the brake until they reached the bottom. It could be done but by the time you … (I MEAN them) got to the bottom the car would be making at least 60 MPH and that road was one big curve. Few made it.

That is a dangerous way to get off the mountain, but I know a young man personally, who found an even more dangerous way to do it and he was filmed on Channel 7 in Lawton skate-boarding down that mountain… and his parents learned about it on the evening news. GROUNDED!!!!

    Getting off the mountain can be dangerous.
        But We Have to do it!
            One Way or Another

              ***

It is good to be on the mountain (in church)…We would like to stay up here out of the trouble in the valley (town)

If we do…. The church will die.
You have a chance to get out there where there is great pain and touch that pain with the Love of
        Jesus Christ our Lord.

Together…….. You have to find the way to bring people to Jesus and to bring Jesus to people…

NOTE: Mountain climbers often tie themselves together by using ropes …. Know Why? "To keep the scared ones from going home.

So… they become a team tied together. If one falls the others THE others "TAKE UP THE SLACK" and save the one who fell.

 Remember the song…Usually sung at Camp…
      "Bind us together with cords that cannot be
        broken?
If we are bound together by these strong cords of love we will be able to minister even to those in the valleys who are in great distress.

Jesus was plainly disgusted with the people who were crowded around and perhaps with the Disciples who had prayed with no success….

But never give up on people in the valley who are in great need of the Gospel of Jesus Christ our Lord...... you may sometimes be disgusted with people too. But never give up on them...
  Invite them again
    Talk to them again...
      Pray for them again...

Don't just invite them... Insist that they come... go get them. Tell them how much they are needed for God's Kingdom's Work here

When they come.... Make sure you have something to feed them... Remember it is Jesus who Restores, Redeems, Saves SO... Get Off the Mountain!

We may enjoy the mountain... but we are called to live and serve in the valley by taking the Light of Christ with us as we leave to face an uncertain world.

This witness is given in the name of Jesus Christ our Lord
Amen!

   It is good to be on the mountain...
    So, we come every Sunday to be on our
      Mountain...

We would like to stay up here out of the trouble in the valley (town) and capture this good feeling...BUT,

There is heartbreak in our Valley...
  There are hurting people all around us
    The needs are staggering

If we do stay on our mountain.... The church will become irrelevant and of no value to the people in the valley...
  (Or just outside our doors)
BUT
Getting off the Mountain
   Can be Dangerous

      ***

NOTE: Mountain climbers often tie themselves together by using ropes .... Know Why?
  "To keep the scared ones from going home.

So... they become a team tied together. If one falls the others THE others "TAKE UP THE SLACK" and save the one who fell.

Remember the song...Usually sung at Camp...
    "Bind us together with cords that cannot be
            broken?

Standing on the Promises
Nehemiah 8:1-4 (RSV)

1. And all the people gathered themselves together as one man into the street that was before the water gate; and they space unto Ezra the scribe to bring the book of the Law of Moses, which the Lord had commanded to Israel.

2. And Ezra the priest brought the law before the congregation both of men and women, and all that could hear with understanding, upon the first day of the seventh month.

3. And he read therein before the street that was before the water gate from the morning until midday, before the men and the women, and those that could understand; and the ears of all the people were attentive unto the book of the law.

4. And Ezra the scribe stood upon a pulpit of wood, which they had made for the purpose....

Ephesians 6:10-18 KJV

10. Finally, my brethren, be strong in the Lord, and in the power of his might.

11. Put on the whole armour of God that ye may be able to stand against the wiles of the devil.

12. For we wrestle not against flesh and blood, but against principalities, against powers, against the rulers of the darkness of this world, against spiritual wickedness in high places.

13. Wherefore take unto you the whole armour of God that ye may be able to withstand in the evil day, and having done all, to stand.

14. Stand therefore, having your loins girt about with truth, and having on the breastplate of righteousness;

15. And your feet shod with the preparation of the gospel of peace;

16. Above all, taking the shield of faith, wherewith ye shall be able to quench all the fiery darts of the wicked.

17. And take the helmet of salvation, and the sword of the Spirit, which is the word of God:

18. Praying always with all prayer and supplication in the Spirit, and watching thereunto with all perseverance and supplication for all saints.

***

Here ends the reading. This is the Word of the Lord.
Thanks be to God! Amen!

AW....Do we have to Stand Up ....AGAIN????

We sing it all the time, don't we? I mean the old favorite song, "Standing on the Promises"
>But have we ever really understood what we are
>>Promising as we sing those words.

I don't think we quite understand the significance of the power of standing upon our feet as a proclamation of what we believe. Let me explain it this way....

Illustration

A mother and her little daughter were having a disagreement. Not too unusual...
>The Mother said: Sit down!
>>The little girl continued to stand...
>I SAID SIT DOWN …..
>>The little girl continued to sand.

Finally the Mother placed both hands on the little girl's shoulders and gently pushed her down, making her sit in her chair…
>But the little girl finally spoke and she said….
>>"Well OK…. But I'm still standing inside…

Note:
We should always remember, and be sensitive for those who are unable to stand. Like the little girl, they do not have to be on their feet to be standing in their hearts.

Proposition

>Have you ever thought about what it means
>>to stand? ....TO TAKE A STAND?

I

Standing may put us in danger

I'm sure you remember the silly old story of the guy with a black eye who was asked how he got it.

He said: "My wife did it. She said Shut up and I thought she said Stand Up".

Where we stand and for what reasons we stand makes a remarkable difference and often has long-term effects on us, and on those we love.

I remember a true, and tragic event of the past.

Seven people died a several years ago at an overlook at Niagara Falls... They didn't think it mattered where they were standing and their guide assured them that everything was secured and that they had nothing to fear, but strong currents of water had undermined the earth beneath the overlook and suddenly the entire structure crashed into the freezing angry waters below... and they all died.

It does matter where and for what we stand.
It is dangerous to stand up in a small boat. Remember the song "Sit Down, Sit Down, you're Rocking the Boat"?

Standing in the middle of a busy street is dangerous too and now it may be getting dangerous to stand up for your beliefs. So... Do we have the courage to do it?

II

Why Do We Stand?

We stand for the National Anthem
     And the Pledge of Allegiance of the Flag
          ....if we are a patriot

We say that we are 'TAKING A STAND" When we are a supporter of something, when we are standing for something.

Remember Moses? We didn't read the scripture but most of you will remember that Moses had walked away from his calling. He had fled the terrible situation of God's people in Egypt and had gone too far places in the desert to become a lonely shepherd, living with the sheep instead of facing his troubles...But God wouldn't let him do that,

...SO, God called him to account ...by causing a bush to catch fire and continue to burn causing Moses to turn aside to see the bush and God Spoke to him from the burning bush, telling him that he was in deed standing on Holy Ground. Moses removed his shoes and stood in that hot, burning sand…. EVER DO THAT?

I have and the Western Oklahoma sand in August could burn like crazy. It was Moses who taught us the value of standing on Holy Ground.

III

We stand because we Reverence Something
    We Stand in the Presence of the Holy God
        And in the presence of God's Word

Nehemiah 8

> 1. *And all the people gathered themselves together as one man into the street that was before the water gate; and they space unto Ezra the scribe to bring the book of the Law of Moses, which the Lord had commanded to Israel.*
> 2. *And Ezra the priest brought the law before the congregation both of men and women, and all that could hear with understanding, upon the first day of the seventh month.*
> 3. *And he read therein before the street that was before the water gate from the morning until midday, before the men and the women, and those that could understand; and the ears of all the people were attentive unto the book of the law.*
> 4. *And Ezra the scribe stood upon a pulpit of wood, which they had made for the purpose….*

Do you know why they were so reverent?
They were hungry for the Word of God. It was the first time they had heard God's word in all the years of their captivity.

Note: I like this... the reader, Ezra, leaned on a pulpit and the people, women, children and the men of Israel, stood ALL MORNING! ...

...and we sometimes complain because we have to stand for the singing of a sacred hymn or the reading of Holy Scripture.

***

At Church Camp and at mealtime… it is not uncommon for the kids to gather outside the dining hall and wait for the appropriate time to enter for the meal…

Often those hungry kids get impatient… especially if the meal is delayed for some unknown reason…

They may start to chant…
> "Here we stand like birds in the wilderness
> Waiting for to be fed…"

THEY ARE STANDING IN EXPECTATION

It is not uncommon these days to see people standing in long lines to get something extremely valuable to those who wait their turn in line. They will stand in line for days, camp out in sleeping bags because they want the latest iPhone, but everybody wants the shortest line at the grocery store.

What then, is the conclusion to all of this? Of course for us it comes from the New Testament reading which tells us in no uncertain terms how and for what we are to take our stand.

Ephesians 6:10-18 (NIV)

10. Finally, be strong in the Lord and in his mighty power.
11. Put on the full armor of God so that you can take your stand against the devil's schemes.
12. For our struggle is not against flesh and blood, but against the rulers, against the authorities, against the powers of this dark world and against the spiritual forces of evil in the heavenly realms.
13. Therefore put on the full armor of God, so that when the day of evil comes, you may be able to stand your ground, and after you have done everything, to stand.
14. Stand firm then, with the belt of truth buckled around your waist, with the breastplate of righteousness in place,
15. And with your feet fitted with the readiness that comes from the gospel of peace.
16. In addition to all this, take up the shield of faith, with which you can extinguish all the flaming arrows of the evil one.
17. Take the helmet of salvation and the sword of the Spirit, which is the word of God.

18. And pray in the Spirit on all occasions with all kinds of prayers and requests. With this in mind, be alert and always keep on praying for all the saints.

  Be strong in the Lord, and in the power of his might.

Put on the whole armour of God that ye may be able to stand against the wiles of the devil.

For we wrestle not against flesh and blood, but against principalities, against powers, against the rulers of the darkness of this world, against spiritual wickedness in high places.

Wherefore take unto you the whole armour of God that ye may be able to withstand in the evil day, and having done all, to stand.

Stand therefore, having your loins girt about with truth, and having on the breastplate of righteousness;

And your feet shod with the preparation of the gospel of peace;

Above all, taking the shield of faith, wherewith ye shall be able to quench all the fiery darts of the wicked.

***

Wow.... What a powerful admonition for us to take our stand against all evil in this world and to stand for all that is good.

Please Stand!

Pastor: Amen!
People: And Amen.

Blessed are Those Who Believe...
John 12:1-8

1. SIX DAYS before the Passover, Jesus came to Bethany, where Lazarus was, whom Jesus had raised from the dead.
2. There they made him a supper; Martha served, and Lazarus was one of those at table with him.
3. Mary took a pound of costly ointment of pure nard and anointed the feet of Jesus and wiped his feet with her hair; and the house was filled with the fragrance of the ointment.
4. But Judas Iscariot, one of his disciples (he who was to betray him), said,
5. "Why was this ointment not sold for three hundred denarii and given to the poor?"
6. This he said, not that he cared for the poor but because he was a thief, and as he had the money box he used to take what was put into it.
7. Jesus said, "Let her alone, and let her keep it for the day of my burial.
8. The poor you always have with you, but you do not always have me."

Mary Believed.

The road for her had not been an easy one.
    Mary, Martha and Lazarus were a strange family...
        It seems that the three siblings were (family)
            It seems that none of them had ever married or
    left home.

Jesus and His Disciples
    Became regular visitors in that home...
        Evidently they were the kind of people who always took
            The preacher in... fed him Sunday dinner and all
            that good
  Stuff...

Mary, and the rest of the family were believers..., that is,
    UNTIL
        JESUS LET THEM DOWN...

        WE REMEMBER THAT EVENT
BEFORE THE READING OF OUR SCRIPTURE TODAY

Lazarus got sick...
>They sent for Jesus... he didn't come immediately.

By the time he got there Lazarus had been in the grave three days....

Mary is angry... Lord if you had been here our Brother would not have died...

You recall the story:
>Jesus went to the tomb
>Jesus asked for it to be opened... they all looked kind of sick and said

"Lord, surely not... BY NOW HE IS ....
>WELL.... YOU DON'T WANT TO GO
>>THERE

JESUS IS TOUCHED WITH THEIR GRIEF
>And .... "JESUS WEPT"!

JESUS CALLS HIM OUT......

And all those gathered around saw it. Some believed, some shook their heads and said "How'd he do it?" and others beat a path back to town to tell the Pharisees who were "out to get Him".

***

Now to our Scripture of the day.
This passage:

FINDS THEM AT HOME...
>MARTHA COOKS,
>>LAZARUS AND GUESTS FEAST...
>>>MARY WASHES JESUS FEET AND POURS OUT
>>>>OINTMENT WORTH
>>>>ABOUT 300 SILVER COINS.....

>And wiped them with her hair.....

JUDAS OBJECTED IMMEDIATELY....

(Rather interesting when you think that he betrayed Jesus for one tenth that amount, 30 pieces of Silver).

Judas Said:
"WHAT A WASTE…. WE COULD HAVE USED THAT MONEY…."
Jesus says a very puzzling thing, that is, puzzling to everyone except Mary, WHO BELIEVED HIM.

Jesus Said:
"LEAVE HER ALONE…. SHE HAS ANNOINTED MY BODY FOR BURIAL IN ADVANCE"….

THE POOR YOU HAVE ALWAYS…. BUT YOU WON'T HAVE ME VERY LONG.

This story is a testimony to Mary's Belief… She REALLY BELIEVED THAT HE WAS GOING TO DIE…
    AND SHE REALLY BELIEVED THAT JESUS WAS THE MESSIAH….

***

There is a sign on Franklin Road WHICH SAYS:
  "Some things have to be BELIEVED,
    To be seen"

EVERYBODY SAW LAZARUS….. But not all believed

MARY BELIEVED AND HER ACTIONS DEMONSTRATED HER BELIEF…..

***

WITHOUT BELIEF
THERE IS NO REVELATION

Some saw all of the events of Jesus' life and believed. They followed him in sincerity …

SOME JUST COULDN'T SEE IT...

We often criticize those who actually saw and heard Jesus in person, saying, "how could they have walked with Jesus saw him perform the miracles and heard his messages about Eternal life, but yet failed to believe.

We fail to take into account that we have the Biblical accounts and are able to compare them with what we know and see from centuries of testimony, yet so many do not accept those accounts and the Biblical record itself and do not believe either.

It is very interesting to me to research the lives of the individual Apostles and try to pinpoint when they actually came to believe, I mean TRULY believe that Jesus was the Messiah. There is no common denominator to say when but it seems to me that the most powerful moments in each of their lives came AFTER CRUCIFIXION AND RESURRECTION.

Poor Old Judas just gave up too quickly.

***

WITHOUT REVELATION THERE IS NO REPENTENCE

True belief puts us on our knees. We, more or less, drop on our knees at the foot of the cross, look fully into the face of Jesus, our Savior, and confess everything we have done, and will do wrong in our lives... Because We Believe!

Repentance is an on-going process because our sinfulness is ongoing. We never conquer or over-come our humanness which is the cause for sinfulness in our very being.

I knew a minister in my teenage years who often greeted his congregation from the pulpit with the words...
    "Good morning Sinners".

That is a little over the top but it did communicate. He also usually proclaimed the love and forgiveness of Jesus Christ our Lord.

Nevertheless, how can we be in the presence of Jesus knowing that his power, love, and compassion for we sinners without truly believing and coming to true and real repentance? We can't! And... truly the cross reminds of the cost of our repentance. It was a high cost and that cost was born solely by Jesus and God, his heavenly Father. Jesus settled that in the agony of the Garden prayer, then faced the cross... ALONE!

***

WITHOUT REPENTANCE
THERE IS NO REAL DEVOTION

Repentance cleanses our soul and all our being. Knowing the forgiveness of Almighty God leads us to a depth of commitment that cannot be understood unless we have experienced it personally.

It is my belief that every person who steps into the sacred desk we call the pulpit, that repentance and forgiveness has brought us there.

A minister I knew was very troubled in his personal life. He always said that he knew he was unworthy to step into that pulpit or preside at the table of the Lord's Supper but he could do it with a clear conscience when he dawned the Robe, the Stoll and prepared himself in prayer. He was right to believe...

None of us, I mean no one that I know, is completely worthy of doing those things for people we know who are like us... "Sinners Saved by Grace". How else are we able to look you, the congregation, in the face?

WITHOUT DEVOTION
THERE IS NO BELIEF AND NO SALVATION

Lucy and Linus, the great theologians are called on again to shed some light on this one....

In a cartoon I seem to remember, Lucy is sick...
   Linus brings her a pillow for her feet
      Chicken soup and hot tea...

I hope that makes you feel better…IS THERE ANYTHING I HAVEN'T THOUGHT OF… he asked.
> LUCY STORMS OUT YES!
>> "PERHAPS YOU HAVEN'T THOUGHT THAT…
>>> I DON'T WANT TO FEEL BETTER".

THERE IS NO HOPE FOR THOSE WHO REFUSE TO BELIEVE.

It is for good reason that Christians are often tagged with the name of "BELIEVERS".
> We have Believers this, and Believers that…
>> Believer s Fellowship
>>> Believers Book Club… etc.

No one dares ask, Believers in What? Everyone knows that to be classified as "A BELIEVER" means that we are believers in Jesus Christ, our Lord. The early church was often called "The Believers".

***

LET US END WHERE WE STARTED

All who truly believe are richly blessed.

That blessing comes silently and mostly unseen by others. I believe that Martha, and even Lazarus did not know the blessing that came to Mary through her act of Belief.

Was not she also one of the Marys who stood at the cross? She was not named as one of them but the accounts of who was there. The several accounts name the ones who stood at the cross as being: Mary, the Mother of Jesus, Mary Magdalene,
Mary the mother of James the Less and Joss, and Salome, who also followed Him and ministered to Him when He was in Galilee; and many other women who came up with Him to Jerusalem.

Scriptures also includes the words…"and many other women who came up with Him to Jerusalem stood afar".

It doesn't matter. MARY, the one who anointed Jesus for his burial BELIEVED! MARY BELIEVED… BLESSED ARE THOSE WHO BELIEVE!

God Leads Us Along
Mark 4:35-41

35. On the same day, when evening had come, He said to them, "Let us cross over to the other side."
36. Now when they had left the multitude, they took Him along in the boat as He was. And other little boats were also with Him.
37. And a great windstorm arose, and the waves beat into the boat, so that it was already filling.
38. But He was in the stern, asleep on a pillow. And they awoke Him and said to Him, "Teacher, do you not care that we are perishing?"
39. Then He arose and rebuked the wind, and said to the sea, "Peace, be still!" And the wind ceased and there was a great calm.
40. But He said to them, "Why are you so fearful? How is it that you have no faith?"
41. And they feared exceedingly, and said to one another, "Who can this be, that even the wind and the sea obey Him!"

There is a song I love… Churches don't sing it much anymore but it says: Pastor, Yoong Kim found it and it was sung beautifully for us this morning. Let me remind us of some of the words, written by G.A. Young. (From Isaiah 43:2) "…when you pass through the waters I will be with you".

Verse 1)
    In shady green pastures, so rich and so sweet,
        God leads His dear children along;
    Where cool waters flow, bathes the weary one's feet
        God leads His dear children along…

Verse 2)
    Sometimes on the mountain…
        Where the sun shines so bright…
        God leads His dear children along;
    Sometimes in the valley… in darkest of night…,
        God leads His dear children along.

Chorus:
    Some thru the waters, some thru the flood,
    Some thru the fire, but all thru the blood.
    Some thru great sorrow, but God gives a song…

...in the night season ... and all the day long.

TRULY GOD LEADS US ALONG

We are standing on a very high mountain...
We are able to see in all directions...!
Our mountain has been built by all of those who have gone before us. ...
From the beginning of time until now...

We are standing on the shoulders of all those who have helped us to arrive here safely...
    On the shoulders of those who taught us about God...
    About Jesus...
    About the faith we have.

Today people in many churches look around from their high mountain ...
to see what other people are doing...
    What other churches are doing...
        And try to do the same... if those churches are

growing....

But we are thankful to be standing where we are... and,
We do not look around to the North or South
 To the East or West....
        But we look UP.... To see the face of God.
 To see where God leads us.

We look down to remember the pathway that brought us here...
    We open the Book that God Gave us...
        And read the words from God's Book...
        And we read the stories.

The Story of Moses

First remember the story of Moses and the Children of Israel...

When I look at the Children of Israel ...
> I am amazed at how God moved them along...
>> From Slavery in Egypt...
>>> Through the Red Sea with Pharaoh's army
>>>> chasing them... and,
God took care of them... and moved them along.

God led them in the daytime with a great cloud...
> At night God led them with a big pillow of fire...

Sometimes they did not want to go... and were rebellious ....
> But God did not give up on them.
>> God does not give up on us either...!

***

When I look at the Cumberland Presbyterian Church ...
> I am amazed at how God has moved us along...

From East Tennessee and Kentucky 200 years ago...
> To take the gospel to many places here...
>> And too far off places all over the world...
>>> God has lead us along...
> To minister to peoples of many nations and languages...
And, God still leads us along.

The Story of Jesus

Now let us remember Jesus... and our Scripture this morning...
> How he led people to go with him....
>> And, how he took care of his Disciples.

Remember how they got into the boat to cross the Sea of Galilee...
> Jesus was asleep in the back of the boat...

They suddenly encountered a BIG storm...
> Called Euroclydon.... An evil wind...
>> It came out of nowhere...

The boat was filling with water....
So, they wake Jesus...

Master, they said, don't you care that we are about to die?
Jesus commanded the wind to cease...
He stretched out his hands and He said...!
Peace! Be Still!

Immediately, the winds died down, and there was a great calm...
Then Jesus said to them:
"Why are you frightened?
Are you without Faith?"...

But they were still afraid...
And asked among themselves,
Who is this man?
Even the waves and the winds obey Him!

The Story of the Disciples

Now let us remember the disciples...
When Jesus stilled the waves, and calmed the waters...
They did not really know him...

This happened very early in the ministry of Jesus...
They did not really get the full picture...
Of where God was leading them...
Until the crucifixion
And the resurrection...
Then they got it,
And when they did it changed everything...
They became strong
They became bold...
They preached with conviction...

God moved them out of their comfort zone...
Too far off places...
Where they proclaimed the story of Jesus...
And won converts (believers) all over the world.

They all paid a great price to follow Jesus…
> They all died terrible deaths as martyrs…, except John,
>> He lived to be very old and wrote letters
>>> About the New Church of Jesus,

The Story of the Church

Now we think about the church of Jesus Christ, Our Lord…
> How it came to us….!

From the time of the Apostles until now…
>>> Storms have beaten against that little church.

The Church has endured persecution…
> The Church has survived wars against her…
>> The Dark Ages tried to kill her and burn the Bibles…
>>> But the Church lives on…

When the church became greedy, domineering…
> And tried to control the world…
God sent the reformers…Who like the Disciples,
> Paid a great price to free the church …
>> From the grips of sinful people.

When the Church came to America…
> The frontier was vast… People scattered everywhere…
>> And lived in isolation… (Log cabins in the woods)
>>> Many had never hear the Gospel…

Out of this grew the Cumberland Presbyterian Church
> With strong desires to reach out …
>> To ever corner of the world…

We are small compared to other Denominations…
> But we are strong in the desire to preach Jesus…

The Story of Your Church

What is the story of your church?
    I do not know the whole story… in fact,
        The story of your church has not been completed.

Remember where we started in this sermon today…
    You are standing on a high mountain.
        You could look in all directions to see what
            others are doing…

But I believe God is calling you to look up… Look at God…
    See what God has done for us…
        Then ask God…,
            Where do you want us to go next?

Conclusion:

Remember our Scripture:
    We are in the same boat together…
        We are followers of Christ…
            The waters can be rough.
    We may encounter the terrible storms like the
        Disciples did….
            But Jesus is in our boat…
Jesus will calm our waters and give us peace…
    Even in the midst of raging storms …

                ***

We live among many people who do not know Jesus.
    We are to invite them into our boat…
        Where Jesus can calm their storms too.
The words of another Hymn come to mind…

Onward, Christian Soldiers
(Verse 3)

Crowns and Thrones may perish, Kingdoms rise and wane…
    But the Cross of Jesus, constant will remain…
Gates of Hell can never, against that Church prevail…
    We have Christ's own promise, and that cannot fail…!

    Remember your mountain…
        Remember Moses
            Remember Jesus and the Disciples
                Remember the Church…

            ***

Look Up for God's leadership!
    Look all around to see where God is leading you …
    And GO!

GO! In the name of the Father, the Sun and the Holy Spirit…
    AMEN!

The Church...At the Gates of Hell
Matthew 16:13-20

For nine years I served on the Board of Trustees of Memphis Theological Seminary. I came to know quite well a Board member by the name of James, a black pastor in Memphis who was also a board member.

Later on, I became director of the Program of Alternate Studies and my office was in the Seminary. When we moved there I was surprised to find James again, not as a board member but as a Doctoral student of MTS, working on his D-Min degree.

If anyone asked him where his church was he would always reply..."It is located between Beal Street and the Grand Central train depot".

If the questioner would say where? James would respond... "It is located at the gates of hell, probably the most dangerous place, and the most crime-ridden place in the city of Memphis".

Note: If you have seen the movie "Blind Side" you will understand what James meant.

James had pulled together a congregation of about 4,000 members and he has coaches working with kids playing street ball of all kinds... He has doctors to treat the sick. Nurses teaching all kinds of groups who will come to learn. There is help for those in any kind of trouble. It is a church located truly where it can do the most good.

Remember the Scripture?

"When Jesus came into the region of Caesarea Philippi," Where? When Jesus came to the very gates of hell on his way toward his own hell on the cross... he came to Caesarea, just up the coast from Jerusalem about 60 miles.

Note: I can't help but wonder why Jesus did that. It was not on his way to anywhere. It was a wicked, perverted city. Obviously nobody there was a follower of Jesus. Jesus is completely unknown there but....
  It was the hometown of Pontius Pilate.

Jesus was totally unknown there but he would someday stand to be judged by their own beloved Pontius Pilate.

The people there who gathered around Jesus were curious and asked… Who is this man?

Jesus turns the question to his Disciples…. What do they say?
Who do they say that I am? They responded, by listening to the crowd there… well, some of them are saying that you are John the Baptist (who had been beheaded) or Elijah, or Jeremiah, or one of the prophets.
    (Is this an affirmation of some kind of belief in   reincarnation?

Again Jesus turns the question on his own followers… "But who do you say that I am? In the midst of that "listening mob" none of the disciples gave a testimony, that is, except the bold one, Simon Peter who finally broke silence and said...
    "… You are the Christ, the Son of the living God."

Verse 17. Jesus answered and said to him, "Blessed are you, Simon Bar-Jonah, for flesh and blood has not revealed this to you, but My Father who is in heaven.

Then came the affirmation that Jesus would build his church on Peter's statement…. Not on Peter…

Verse 18. "And I also say to you that you are Peter, and on this rock I will build my church, and the gates of Hades shall not prevail against it.

Of course Jesus knew the trials and tribulations of the church that would be formed on this statement and he made a solemn promise that the true church would not be brought down, even by the gates of hell.

I

Please know that were ever the true church of Jesus Christ is located today, it is located at the very gates of hell. But that is exactly where we can do the most good.

God help us when we flea from the gates of hell to try to go minister in the safe places, the rich places, the peaceful places.

We don't have to live at the doorway of the ghetto to be living at the very gates of hell. Our beautiful suburbs are just as sinful as the rotten ghettos of our most wicked cities. The church is stationed where it is in order to serve…
> In order to serve those close to us, or
> To serve those who come from afar…

This Church is not a community church, we are what is called a regional church, drawing membership from several miles away from our community. But that does not mean that we are excused from ministering to our communities… be they near or far,
> Be they Black, Hispanic, White, Asian or a mixture of all   cultures.

Remember my friend James?

He would weep as he spoke of young people already trapped in Dope, Drugs, and illicit sexual activities by the time they are in Jr. High school, caught up in prostitution and drug running by the time they are out of grade school.

II

Now a question is thrown at our feet.
We are Disciples aren't we?
What do you think? Who is this Jesus?
What can he do for the church at the gates of Hell?

I believe the cross is looming ahead of Jesus… it is on his mind. It is a threat for him to push on, and to make his disciples stand on their own testimony. To make them ready.

It is no less for us. Jesus pushes us on toward the cross of our own decisions and commitment.

Jesus demands:
> A commitment from those bewildered disciples that will   take them to the very foot of the cross and then on beyond   to the churches they will build and the places they will   serve.

Jesus demands:
> A commitment from us. He continues to say to us. Make up your minds. Affirm your faith. Stand with me. Serve with me.

Are you quitting? Are you giving up? Are you just   marking time until we have to close the doors instead of reaching out the lost.

So, what is our affirmation?
    "THAT JESUS CHRIST IS LORD TO THE GLORY OF
    GOD THE FATHER…."

III

Do we believe?
That Jesus Christ and His Church Will Stand
Against the very gates of Hell…?

I know many people whose lives have been transformed,
    Made new,
        Set free by the power of Christ through His
    Church.
    They have been transformed
Saved, and changed by the power of Christ through his Church.

I know many people who are standing in dangerous places,
    Doing ministry and witness
    Where it is not popular to do so…
We pray for missionaries on foreign soil
    Doing dangerous service…and we should never forget to   pray for them,
  …but there are people much closer to us who are doing
   The same

Some of you will know Walter Smith

I have known Walter for about 25 years but I did not know, until I visited the General Assembly of the Cumberland Presbyterian Church in America when it met just across from St. Frances Hospital a few years ago that a terrible thing had happened to Walter.

He and I renewed our old acquaintance at that Assembly. He told me the whole story of what had happened to him and what was happening to him now.

He is pastor of Tulsa Mission Cumberland Presbyterian Church, Just off of North Cincinnati Street.

He is serving in a dangerous community. When I saw him at their General Assembly Walter came up to me with that same old smile. As we re-made our acquaintance after some 15 years Walter told me what had happened to him and his church.

Young children would walk past his church cursing at him and telling him to get out of their community and leave them alone.
Then one night about 3:00 AM there was a drive by shooting. Walter was hit three times… almost died and after a long recuperation, he is back in his pulpit and back to his community.

His Affirmation:

"I'm not leaving… the gates of Hell cannot prevail against the church of Jesus Christ our Lord."
    Pray for them…
     Reach out to them…
       They are serving at the very gates of Hell,
And so are we.
    In fact, every church that is going what it ought to be doing is actually serving at the very gates of Hell, and it matters not where that church is located. The gates of Hell are as present in the affluent communities as in the ghetto. The sins just take different forms.

Conclusion

Now comes the question again… the question Jesus asked his puzzled disciples… WHO DO YOU SAY THAT I AM?

    Well… I presume that most of us have settled that question and that we have said that Jesus Christ is our Lord and our Savor, but there is another question staring us in the face too.

Are we willing to join others who are standing every day against violence, against community crime?
    Against crimes against our children…
  Against evil of all kinds and in all places.

If our Church does this the Church wins.
    Our profession is true,

And we are truly standing at the very gates of Hell with a message of salvation that shall touch the hearts, minds, and lives of those who would be lost without our witness.

>This church and every church
>>Is located at the strategic place of service to
>>>A lost and sinful world.

Now, continue to seek, as you have been seeking, the direction
Of ministries you can do to fulfill your calling.

In the Name of Jesus Christ our Lord… AMEN!

Jesus, the Shepherd King
(Christ the King Sunday)
Matthew 25:31-46

31. "When the Son of Man comes in His glory, and all the holy angels With Him, then He will sit on the throne of His glory.

32. "All the nations will be gathered before Him, and He will separate them one from another, as a shepherd divides his sheep from the goats.

33. "And He will set the sheep on His right hand, but the goats on the left.

34. "Then the King will say to those on His right hand, `Come, you blessed of My Father, inherit the kingdom prepared for you from the foundation of the world:

35. `For I was hungry and you gave me food; I was thirsty and you gave me drink; I was a stranger and you took me in;

36. `I was naked and you clothed me; I was sick and you visited me; I was in prison and you came to me.'

37. "Then the righteous will answer Him, saying, `Lord, when did we see you hungry and feed you, or thirsty and give you drink?

38. `When did we see you a stranger and take you in, or naked and clothe you?

39. `Or when did we see you sick, or in prison, and come to you?'

40. "And the King will answer and say to them, `Assuredly, I say to you, inasmuch as you did it to one of the least of these my brethren, you did it to me.'

41. "Then He will also say to those on the left hand, `Depart from me, you cursed, into the everlasting fire prepared for the devil and his angels:

42. `For I was hungry and you gave me no food; I was thirsty and you gave me no drink;

43. `I was a stranger and you did not take me in, naked and you did not clothe me, sick and in prison and you did not visit Me.'

44. "Then they also will answer Him, saying, `Lord, when did we see you hungry or thirsty or a stranger or naked or sick or in prison, and did not minister to you?'

45. "Then He will answer them, saying, `Assuredly, I say to you, inasmuch as you did not do it to one of the least of these, you did not do it to Me.'

46. "And these will go away into everlasting punishment, but the righteous into eternal life."

Story:

An older minister was sweeping leaves off the long flite of church steps early on Sunday morning…

An older lady approached… needing help with the steps, and as he
Was assisting her up the steps…
 She looked at him and said…
      WHO ARE YOU?

HE SAID: I am the new pastor of visitation….
She Said: Who is preaching this morning?
HE SAID: (with a bit of pride in his voice) Well, I am…

She paused about half way up the steps and looked him over and said
     In that case…

    WOULD YOU HELP ME BACK DOWN THOSE STEPS?

Some of you didn't know who was preaching this morning but I am not going to help any of you back down those steps until the service is over.

Prayer for Enlightenment:

    Come, Holy Spirit:
        Come as the wind and Cleanse…
        Come as the Fire and Burn…
        Come as the Light and Reveal….
    Convict… Consecrate… Cleanse

Until we are wholly Thine….

Do We Have a King?

This is Christ the King Sunday, but did Jesus Christ, our Lord really want to be a king like King David?

When America won our independence from England, we declared that we had no king.

When people were gathered in the hall of Pilate, shouting for the execution of Jesus, they declared...
    WE HAVE NO KING BUT CESAR....

Perhaps a better approach would be to proclaim Jesus as our Shepherd King. In fact, Jesus came to be the Messiah, and the Jewish people had in mind a KING LIKE DAVID....

HOWEVER, Jesus proclaims himself as
    The Great Shepherd...
        Until the time of judgment...

THEN... he proclaims that he is the righteous judge...
    Sitting on his throne and judging all
    Nations.

EXEGESIS

All eyes are on Jesus:
    They want him to spell out what will happen in the
End of things... and Jerusalem would soon be destroyed in about 35 years...

JESUS SPEAKS TO THEM IN PARABLES...
    ... Telling them that the day and hour are known
        Only by GOD

Jesus Speaks of the importance of KEEPING WATCH:
    Wedding (10 brides maids)
        Parable of the Talents...
            AND NOW A SHEPHERD...

  A SHEPHERD WHO IS ALSO KING
"When the Son of man shall come in his glory with all his holy Angels and sit on the throne... he shall judge all nations...

SO.... Jesus is our SHEPHARD KING
    (Our Shepherd and our King)

I

JESUS OUR SHEPHERD

The Sheep know the Shepherd's Voice…
    Hundreds of sheep were sent out to graze each morning.
    Each Shepherd was sent out with 100 sheep
    Each Shepherd had a distinctive call…

He could gather his sheep from the mix by calling
    Them to himself…

At evening time he counted the 100 back into the sheepfold.
    If one was missing he left the 99 to look for the
    One lost sheep…

The Shepherd's Crook… pulled the unruly one out of trouble.

THE SHEPHERD WINDOW… at old Daingerfield Church…
    A Tiffany Window…
    Shepherd holding a lamb with a bandaged leg…

THE UNRULY LAMB….
    Wolf bate…
        Danger of death…
            Shepherd was responsible…

SOLUTION: Break the front fore-paw and bind it up
    In a splint… BUT IF HE DOES…
    He has to carry that Lamb until his leg is healed…

RESULT…. That lamb is forever attached to that shepherd
    Like a faithful puppy…

Now does that song "Praise Him, Praise Him" take on a new?
Meaning?
  "…like a shepherd Jesus will guard his children…
    In His arms he carries them all day long…:

THAT IS US…

II

JESUS OUR SAVIOUR

This life is filled with much heart-break for most of us. When those things come to us we will react in a number of possible ways…
    …but mostly we will react in one of two ways because
    We are believers.

We will either Run away from our shepherd and hide in the brambles….
   OR
We will come to our shepherd for healing and comfort.

III

JESUS OUR KING
KNOWS THE SHEEP FROM THE GOATS

JESUS CAME TO SAVE US FROM:
FAULTY SHEPHERDS

Faulty Shepherds (Scribes and Pharisees) had damaged Israel beyond repair.

God sent his Son in the fullness of time… not only to save Israel, but to save us.

Conclusion

YES… WE DO HAVE A KING

KING OF MY LIFE
I CROWN THEE NOW
THINE SHALL THE GLORY BE
LEST I FORGET THY THORN CROWNED BROW.
LEAD ME TO CALVARY

We do have a King,
Jesus who died for us

And sits as King
At the right hand of God our Father
Pleading for us.

HE IS OUR SHEPHERD AND HE KNOWS US
    HE LOVES US
        HE DIED FOR US…

AND… FOR ALL WHO WILL FOLLOW HIM.

There are many sheep wandering away from the Shepherd.
There are many wounded ones out there
There are many lost ones out there…

Dare we pray the penitent's prayer….?

    "O Lord, if there be any wicked way in me…

    Break Me!
        Heal Me
            Until I am Completely Yours…

If we are trying to be like Jesus in our Christian Walk we will remember what Jesus calls us to do, and we will…

    Loves the sheep
        Will fight off the wolves for the Sheep
            Will bind up their wounds and carry them
                Will search for the lost.

In the Name of the Father the Son and the Holy Spirit. Amen!

Take Care of What God Gives You
Joshua 24:13-17 (NIV)

13. So I gave you a land on which you did not toil and cities you did not build; and you live in them and eat from vineyards and olive groves that you did not plant.'

14. "Now fear the LORD and serve him with all faithfulness. Throw away the gods your forefathers worshiped beyond the River and in Egypt, and serve the LORD.

15. But if serving the LORD seems undesirable to you, then choose for yourselves this day whom you will serve, whether the gods your forefathers served beyond the River, or the gods of the Amorites, in whose land you are living. But as for me and my household, we will serve the LORD."

16. Then the people answered, "Far be it from us to forsake the LORD to serve other gods!

17. It was the LORD our God himself who brought us and our fathers up out of Egypt, from that land of slavery, and performed those great signs before our eyes. He protected us on our entire journey and among all the nations through which we traveled.

When the Children of Israel made it to the Promised Land… they thought all of their problems were solved forever.

Well… is that true?

When America won her independences from King George… they perhaps thought likewise…

They have given us a great gift but that gift has been bought with the blood and commitment of thousands before us and we have to take care of this fragile UNION…

IN OUR SCRIPTURE…..
    Moses is dead… God took him and he was not allowed to enter into this Promised Land.

    Joshua is their new leader but he has to know that he can count on them to face their difficulties…

THE TEST….. DO YOU THINK YOU CAN LIVE UP TO WHAT GOD IS REQUIRING…….?

PEOPLE: "We will serve the Lord…..
       Forsake our Idles….
              We will never again serve false gods...

Take Care
      Of what God gives you

Everything we have is a gift from God

That gift is represented in the Land in which we live and has been bought with a high price

      Our land
           Our homes
                Our families
                      Our heritage
                          Our Freedom
    AND OUR FUTURE.

                ***

TAKE CARE OF THE LAND

Our roots are in the land. Not many remain on the land as farmers to take care of us and feed us. But our very lively hood depends on the land.

We are Stewards of the land…. But we have become a wasteful people.

I REMEMBER MY OWN ROOTS
IN THE LAND

My Dad, (Preacher Farmer) taught and preached
   (After the dust bowl) that
   If you fail to take care of the soil you die…
                    Or go to California with the rest   of the Okies and (Aries).

This Dust-Bowl Farmer watched helplessly as his crops were swept clean from the fields by the strong burning winds

    Cutting sand
        And Grasshoppers devouring what was left.

How could he feed his family....? The dust bowl made farming and cattle totally non-productive, but Dad was always creative. So, he sold roofing even though there were not many buyers.

He placed a bid on the courthouse roof at Cordell, Washita County, Oklahoma and got the bit. The only catch was that he had to install it. My older Brother, then 22 years old and a friend, Warren Jackson were elected to install the copper roofing on the four clocks of that beautiful building. That was in 1937. They just replaced that copper roof this year (2012).

With conservation and Stewardship of the land came many attempts to make sure the dust bowl didn't happen again and there was government money for creative people.

Cotton fields were limited in the number of acres that could be allotted to the farmers. Dad got the job of measuring cotton land.

Erosion was a big factor in the disaster of the dust bowl and there was work to be done to help take care of the land. Dad bought and used the first terracing machine and BUILT THE FIRST TERRACES IN Western Oklahoma Taking care of the land.

NOW, HOW DO WE TAKE CARE OF WHAT GOD HAS GIVEN US?

WE HONOR THE SACRIFICES OF OTHERS!

World War II led to the greatest number of sacrifices our world has ever seen....
    HISTORY TEACHES ONLY PART OF THE STORY…

The evil axis of powers exterminated
    6 million Jews….
        The Sacrifices of US and Allied Troops
            12 Million….died…for our freedom

Of Course you have been reminded of this Sacrifice in such movies as, The Longest Day and Saving Private Ryan.
That "Longest Day" remains in my memory as a Child…. When we heard from this invasion by the old battery operated Radio….

JUNE 6TH 1944, D-DAY, OMAHA BEECH
    (German stronghold on that Beech)

    General in Command of the entire operation was Dwight. D. Eisenhower who reportedly did not sleep all that night. How could he?

Clouds had hidden the enormous fleet of American ships ready to unload the waiting invading troops at dawn.
Eisenhower prayed! (Along with everyone else who knew).

    They prayer FOR THE CLOUDS TO LIFT
        AND TO SURPRISE THE GERMANS
            BOTH OCCURRED……….!

WHEN THE CLOUDS LIFTED
    THE GERMAN COMMAND REPORTEDLY SAID…
        "THIS IS IMPOSSIBLE"……….

THE AMERICAN COMMANDERS KNEW THE COST
    Watched landing crafts blown out of the water
        Killing 40 men at a time …

Thousands killed before they hit the beech…
(What if they had weakened …...)

BUT THEY STAYED THE COURSE AND WATCHED PERHAPS THE WORST CARNAGE IN THE HISTORY OF THE WORLD….

    9,386 young American Men died that day for US….
     I was nine…
        Many of you were not yet born…..
            But they died for you and me…………
    33 pairs of brothers
    33 American households lost TWO SONS THAT DAY.

WITH THEIR LIFE'S BLOOD THEY GAVE US OUR FREEDOM….
BUT WILL WE TAKE CARE OF WHAT GOD HAS
GIVEN US THROUGH THEIR SACRIFICE….
ON MANY BATTLEFIELDS…?
    Such as, Korea,
        Viet Nam,
            add even the battles going on NOW.

JOSHUA TURNED TO THE PEOPLE AND SAID….
    Moses had led you thus far.
        God has given you the land ….

    IF…… IF….YOU WILL TURN YOUR BACKS ON YOUR IDOLS AND WORSHIP THE LORD, YOUR GOD….

That day, that very hour the people waiting to enter the "promised land" made a covenant with Almighty God to keep the laws and statutes set before them in the Ten Commandments.

Of course it would not be long before they broke that covenant and had to pay the price by being taken captives into a far off land where they would be slaves and servants to people rather than serving God.

***

AMERICA! We need to remember that mostly we are people of faith and that God has continued to remind us:

    That if we keep the covenants of Holy Scripture
    That if we take care of what God has given us, through
        The sacrifices of Jesus Christ our Lord, and,
        Through the sacrifices of countless others
        Who gave the intimate gift?
    Then we are being good stewards and that we are

TAKING CARE OF WHAT GOD HAS GIVEN US.

REMEMBER…. MOST OF ALL…. THE SACRIFICIAL GIFT OF JESUS CHRIST OUR LORD.
    Pastor: Amen!
    People: And Amen.

Behold the Lamb of God
(A service of Holy Communion)
Revelation 1:4-8

1:4). I John, to the seven churches which are in Asia: Grace to you and peace from Him who is and who was and who is to come, and from the seven Spirits who are before His throne,
…. and from Jesus Christ, the faithful witness, the firstborn from the dead, and the ruler over the kings of the earth.
To Him who loved us and washed us from our sins in His own blood, and has made us kings and priests to His God and Father, to Him be glory and dominion forever and ever. Amen.
Behold, He is coming with clouds, and every eye will see Him, and they also who pierced Him. And all the tribes of the earth will mourn because of Him. Even so, Amen.
8. "I am the Alpha and the Omega, the Beginning and the End," says the Lord, "who is and who was and who is to come, the Almighty."
Here ends the Reading...

> *This IS the Word of the Lord*
> *Thanks be to God....AMEN!*

When Jesus started calling his Disciples he encountered a young man named John... the youngest of the Disciples.

It is most likely, and we will assume, that this is the same John writing again about Jesus, the Lamb of God.

When John was exiled on the Island of Patmos he had only one person as his constant companion...
Jesus, the Lamb of God...

John is 90 years old.
> He loves Jesus with the depth of all his
> Years and now in exile.

Let us remember what John said in the beginning of his relationship with Jesus and now at the end of his life citing a Flashback in John's Memory:

St. John 1:29 (NKJV) The next day John saw Jesus coming toward him, and said, "Behold! The Lamb of God who takes away the sin of the world!

He says: Revelation 1:3 (NKJV)
"Blessed is he who reads and those who hear the words of this prophecy, and keep those things which are written in it; for the time is near.
John is able to get this message out to the outside world... (Or we would never have read it).

TO THE CHURCHES....AND TO US...

He writes: about the Lamb:

> He loves us:
> He has made us a Kingdom of Priests:
> He is coming on the Clouds
> He is the Alpha and the Omega

The beginning and the end.....

He loves us!

> The real question is ...
> > Just how much do we love Him?

As we come to this communion table we know that...
> Jesus Christ, our Lord
> > Loved us enough to die for us...

Perhaps John is reflecting on the time with Jesus when Jesus was making preparation for the horrible days ahead and to help those disciples prepare for what was ahead for all of them, and John remembers:

JOHN 14:

He prepared the way for us to follow him
> He promised to return for us
> > He has prepared a place for us.

The love of Jesus Christ our Lord has been seen, known, and experienced by most every one of us who gather to worship Him here. We have experienced the love of Jesus.

Now we must ask ourselves...
> BUT HOW MUCH DO WE LOVE HIM?

II

He has made us a Kingdom of Priests:

NO MORE HEBREW PRIESTS.....
> NO MORE HEIRARCHY
>> NO SANHEDRIN WHO KILLED JESUS

WE ARE ALL EQUIL BEFORE GOD

As you continue in your ministry and as a church involved in ministry ...REMEMBER,

The preacher is NOT the authority...
> DO This... Do that!

We are all equal at the Lord's Table.
> The pastor and elders preside,
>> But all are ministers, serving one another.

We often practice the serving of Holy Communion in different ways, but remember as we take Holy Communion this morning we shall take the elements from the hand of the serving Elder, present it to the next person sitting beside us, who will take it and pass it on to others, and in so doing we are becoming the servant / priest.

This passage of Scripture assures us that God is in control of this troubled universe and at the will of God, and in God's time, this Jesus who is standing with John on Patmos, will return.

III

Jesus is coming on the Clouds

This old world is in a mess.
> Jesus taught us that He would return at a time when
>> no one was ready... and we seem to be getting to that place in a hurry, when very few people seem to
>>> believe that Jesus will come again.

Jesus will return so that:
    All flesh shall see it together...

John says that we shall all Behold Him, meaning that the whole earth and all the people in it will not be able to dismiss it. Everyone will know and see this.

Does Scripture not say many times, that truly ...
    "ALL FLESH shall see it, together?

Now recall the first part of this scripture:

Rev: 1-4 "I John, to the seven churches which are in Asia: Grace to you and peace from Him who is and who was and who is to come, and from the seven Spirits who are before His throne..."

Recall with me the fact that he is speaking a strong message to the Seven Churches of Asia..... And consequently, to us, saying, BE READY!

IV

He is the Alpha and the Omega

The beginning and the End...
    He is coming soon....
        And, we are challenged to be prepared, and to
        BE READY.

We are also challenged by the presence of Christ at this table to not only Remember Jesus at this supper but to make new and continued commitment to be servants and priests to those who do not know Him.

We are certainly challenged to stand firm in our convictions as Christians and as the Church of Jesus Christ our Lord.

Confession swells over us when we know that often we have not stood against the overwhelming changes in our society. The church, as well as every one of us as individuals, often take the easy way out and do not put ourselves on the line for what we know the Holy Scriptures call us to stand for.

Illustration:

A story of a Young Roman Soldier who had been a coward in battle. He was being tried for Cowardice but was granted a hearing in the presence of the Emperor, Alexander.

As he stood there in embarrassment, knowing that he surely would be sentenced to die...

The Emperor said: WHAT IS YOUR NAME?

The young man shamefully answered...
    My name is Alexander... Same as yours.

The Emperor was Angry but decided to be lenient to this young man.... HE SAID:
    Change your Name....
        Or Change your Allegiance.

NOW...LET US PLEDGE OUR ALLEGIANCE TO THE ONE WE SERVE AS LORD....

OUR ALLEGIANCE IS TO THE
    LAMB... OF GOD....

REMEMBER THE WORDS WHEN YOU JOINED THIS CHURCH? "WHO IS YOUR LORD AND SAVIOR?"

And you answered: "JESUS IS LORD".
    As you come to this table...

Or as you reach your hand to take the elements that represent the Body and Blood of Jesus Christ, our Lord. You pledge again that Jesus Christ is your Lord and Savior...

BEHOLD THE LAMB OF GOD!

    Pastor: Amen!
    People: And Amen.

www.ingramcontent.com/pod-product-compliance
Lightning Source LLC
Chambersburg PA
CBHW052156110526
44591CB00012B/1975